Oliphant's Presidents

Twenty-five Years of Caricature

OLIPHANT'S PRESIDENTS

Text by

WENDY WICK REAVES

Foreword by PAT OLIPHANT
Introduction by ALAN FERN

Organized by

ART SERVICES INTERNATIONAL, Alexandria, Virginia, in conjunction with

THE NATIONAL PORTRAIT GALLERY, Smithsonian Institution, Washington, D.C.

Published by

ANDREWS AND McMEEL, A Universal Press Syndicate Company
Kansas City • New York

Pat Oliphant is represented by the Susan Conway Carroll Gallery, Washington, D.C.

Pat Oliphant's editorial cartoons are distributed internationally by Universal Press Syndicate.

The exhibition was organized by Art Services International, Alexandria, Virginia, in conjunction with The National Portrait Gallery, Smithsonian Institution, Washington, D.C., and is circulated by Art Services International.

Library of Congress Cataloging in Publication Data

Reaves, Wendy Wick, 1950–
    Oliphant's presidents: twenty-five years of caricature by Pat Oliphant / Wendy Wick Reaves; foreword by Pat Oliphant; introduction by Alan Fern.
       p.   cm.
    "The exhibition was organized by Art Services International, Alexandria, Virginia, in conjunction with the National Portrait Gallery, Smithsonian Institution, Washington, D.C."—T.p. verso.
    ISBN 0-8362-1813-2 : $12.95
    1. United States—Politics and government—1945-　—Caricatures and cartoons—Exhibitions.　2. Presidents—United States—Caricatures and cartoons—Exhibitions.　3. American wit and humor, Pictorial—Exhibitions.　4. Oliphant, Pat, 1935-　—Exhibitions.
    I. Oliphant, Pat, 1935-　.　II. Art Services International.
    III. National Portrait Gallery (Smithsonian Institution)　IV. Title.
    E839.5.R37　1990　　　　　　　　　　　89-78355
    973.92'092'2—dc20　　　　　　　　　　CIP

Editor: Nancy Eickel
Photographer: Rolland White
Designer: Stephen Kraft

CONTENTS

ACKNOWLEDGMENTS

In today's world of rapid communication, we hear of events from around the world as they unfold. With this overwhelming influx of news and facts comes the need to sort out the information and to put it in perspective. Teams of television anchormen and news reporters attempt to do so each day, but rarely does a single individual manage to distill important occurrences—much less the character and appearance of the prominent players—to their essence. Pat Oliphant is a master of this art.

For twenty-five years, Oliphant has produced remarkable political cartoons that have both reflected and shaped public opinion. His drawings have affected the way we view our presidents and their handling of national and international affairs. As this exhibition and catalogue confirm, some, if not much, of our reaction to the chief executive has been influenced by Oliphant's caricatures and drawings.

We are indebted to Pat Oliphant for his support and encouragement in coordinating this exhibition. He lent freely both of his time and his collection to make this presentation possible. We are also grateful for his characteristically stimulating writing in the catalogue's foreword. It is an honor to know and work with him.

We at Art Services International thank the National Portrait Gallery for its valuable collaboration in organizing *Oliphant's Presidents*. In particular, we commend Wendy Wick Reaves, Curator of Prints and Drawings, for her inspired selection of works and for her insightful essay. We also acknowledge Dr. Alan Fern, Director, for his support of this project from the outset and for his informative introduction. The assistance of Beverly J. Cox, Nello Marconi, and Rolland White is greatly appreciated as well.

Special thanks are extended to Susan Conway Carroll for her enthusiasm and expert help at every turn. Not only has she been a major force behind the success of this presentation, but she also has been most generous—through the Susan Conway Carroll Gallery—in assisting with the loan of so many exceptional pieces to this traveling exhibition. It is also a pleasure to acknowledge the other lenders for their generosity: the Western Historical Collections of the University of Colorado at Boulder, Larry L. King and Barbara S. Blaine, Raymond C. Weigel, the National Trust for Historic Preservation, and Pat Oliphant, through Art Wood and the Susan Conway Carroll Gallery.

This catalogue has been made possible by the support of Andrews and McMeel. We extend our personal thanks to Thomas N. Thornton, President, and to Donna Martin, Vice-President, for their assistance during the catalogue's production. In addition, we are grateful to Nancy Eickel for her skillful editing and to Stephen Kraft for his handsome catalogue design.

Finally, we send our thanks to the staff of Art Services International, in particular Marcene Edmiston, Elizabeth Hooper, and Sally Thomas, for seeing to the myriad details of the exhibition and tour.

LYNN KAHLBER BERG
Director

JOSEPH W. SAUNDERS
Chief Executive Officer

Art Services International

FOREWORD

In the mid–1930s, the renowned British cartoonist David Low was sketching from life a pompous group of top-hatted gentlemen as they emerged in high collars and frock coats from an emergency session of the League of Nations, where they had been deliberating on the proper punishment to be meted out to Mussolini for his recent incursions in Abyssinia. An acquaintance of Low's, seeing what the artist was doing, leaned close and remarked, "Mr. Low, henceforth photography will suffice." His point is well taken, and perhaps he was right.

In thirty-five odd years of watching and caricaturing public figures, I have increasingly felt that the figures are lampooning themselves and that the business of satire is continually and deliberately being undercut by the subjects. How else to explain the spectacle of Lyndon Baines Johnson picking up his dogs by the ears or hoisting his shirt to show his operation scar to the press? How else to account for the thespian furtiveness (which, after all, was no act) of Richard Nixon, or why Gerald Ford was in imminent danger of falling over or banging his head the moment he stood up? How else to justify Jimmy (a grown man called Jimmy) Carter finding the Killer Rabbit, or the public tolerating the goofy vacuity of Ronald Reagan, who drew his every movement and utterance from old B-movie scripts? And how else to reconcile the Yankee WASP George Bush with the Texan George Bush, or any other George Bush?

Life is kind to cartoonists, as least in their working life, and in this country it is especially true. I owe America so much for providing such a beautiful and varied canvas as a backdrop and then peopling the foreground with a rich, almost overabundance of charlatans of all shades—wonderful Barnum politicians of varying degrees of shamelessness, cabinet opportunists, self-aggrandizing public servants, shiftless bureaucrats, and assorted lickspittles, greedmongers, and common thieves—all of them exciters of the linkage between brain and drawing hand. If photography alone sufficed fifty or more years ago, then television in this age should suffice doubly so, and this art by now should have disappeared.

Furthermore, this mode of expression also faces the threat of an always diminishing field of reference. In fairly recent memory, allusions to works by Shakespeare and other fuddy-duddies were recognized and accepted as suitable vehicles for satiric opinion—but no more. The riches of literature, along with the lessons of history, have been largely ignored by present educators. The symbols of Aesop lie fallow, as do the titles and imagery of Poe, Hemingway, Kipling, Twain, and all the others. No more "Alas, poor Yorick! I knew him. . . ."

No more ravens quothing "Nevermore!" Barely a "Farewell to Arms" left in the house. Send not to see for whom the bell tolls. It tolls for an education system that has sold out. Products of such a system are not likely to savor a cartoon that relies for its impact on the follies of today juxtaposed against those of fifty, fifteen, or even five years ago. Without reference there are no parameters; without parameters, no perspective; and without perspective, alas, no satire.

Cartooning and caricature, however, offer more than the photographic image or the fleeting electronic signal. A strong audience exists that needs to hold in the hand and contemplate a graphic distillation of the personality of the strutting popinjay on last night's news. This audience wants a visual rendering of immediacy and endurance that can be cut from the printed page and saved on the refrigerator, or if disliked, can be ripped from the page, have rude recommendations scrawled upon it, and mailed back to the artist. Such people, pro and con, possess awareness and opinion, and as such are to be blessed.

It is my contention, having said all this, that cartoonists should be seen and not heard. I find myself largely unable to discuss my own work, and I dread artists who drape their work in verbiage to disguise its shortcomings. English ladies, it is said, wear shoes that appear to have been built by someone who has only heard shoes described. In my case, to discuss a cartoon or caricature is to destroy it, for without the visual component the piece ends up sounding like English ladies' shoes.

There are, thank goodness, those more learned than I who can, and do, describe my function and my work with the assurance of instructors and scholars, and I yield to them in true fascination. For me, however, this art of the daily deadline leaves me only as good as I was yesterday, and the work itself, good or bad, is that which must suffice.

PAT OLIPHANT

INTRODUCTION

It is a pleasure to introduce this collection of Pat Oliphant's presidential portrayals. In the 1970s, when I was working at the Library of Congress, not far from the newspaper that employed him as political cartoonist, Oliphant and I met for lunch on occasion. I recall those meetings happily. For a man whose acerbic visual comments were powerful irritants to political figures around the globe, Oliphant in person proved to be a surprisingly agreeable fellow, and a lasting acquaintance. Even when we had not met for a while, we quickly picked up where we had left off the last time, complaining about the world, worrying about the permanence of materials he was using, and exchanging views about art in general and satire in particular. While not without a strong sense of his own capabilities, he is open in his admiration for his predecessors in the field, and we often went back to the Library to look at original drawings by great cartoonists of the past. He has a refreshing informality (one of the winning qualities of Australians, in general) and an outspoken scorn of pretension. He also possesses a poet's economy of language and a great gift for the telling phrase. His cartoons benefit almost as much from his abilities as a writer as from his pungent and animated draughtsmanship.

These lines are being written on the twenty-fifth anniversary of Oliphant's move to the United States, as we prepare to celebrate this milestone with an exhibition of his drawings and sculpture that record each of the presidents who led this country since his arrival. He moved to America to replace Paul Conrad as political cartoonist for *The Denver Post* and quickly established himself as a major talent among American newspaper cartoonists in the midst of the 1964 presidential campaign. From 1965, his drawings were internationally syndicated by the Los Angeles Times Syndicate, and a year later he was influential enough to be awarded a Pulitzer Prize. As his career has unfolded, he has continued to gather honors steadily, ranging from a Sigma Delta Chi award to an honorary degree from Dartmouth.

Oliphant was born in 1935 in Adelaide, Australia. After finishing school, he started working as a copy boy on *The Adelaide News*, moving shortly to *The Adelaide Advertiser* in the same capacity; soon he joined the art department of the *Advertiser* and before long became its political cartoonist. He worked in Denver until *The Washington Star* hired him in 1975. When the *Star* folded in 1981, he continued to draw his daily cartoons for international syndication on a free-lance basis. Today he is represented by the Universal Press Syndicate.

Oliphant's craft—the depiction of well-known leaders in political cartoons—is such a familiar feature of our everyday life that it is taken for granted. Most newspapers, and even some magazines, reserve a space on the editorial page or the op-ed page facing it for a visual comment on the events of the moment, and these events are usually centered around the character and personalities of the international, national, and local celebrities who must be measured by their behavior as they face issues. Yet the political cartoon as we know it occupies a comparatively recent place in the history of the visual arts, partly because the illustrated newspaper is only a bit over a century old and partly because most visual satirists before the eighteenth century were concerned with other targets.

The ancient Egyptian or Greek artist was primarily devoted to the depiction of the human ideal or to the rendition of the gods in a humanly recognizable form. They could not help noticing that actual people often fell far short of the ideal forms celebrated in painting and sculpture, or that human expressions and gestures sometimes called to mind the appearance and behavior of beasts. The converse was equally compelling: the faces and postures of animals often seemed to mimic human physiognomy and human action. This gave rise to a sub-class of art in which human behavior was commented upon by depicting people with animal heads or bodies, thus underscoring the unlovely, accidental qualities that most people embody.

Animals have long found a place in the political cartoon. While Aesop and the Bible provided abundant sources for narrative analogies and furnished the artist with scores of ways to relate animal behavior to the human condition, other artists preferred to build on the ages-old search for physiognomic similarities between people and animals. If at first this was merely a delight in putting such characterizations as "horse face" into visual terms, soon the qualities popularly associated with animals—rabbits as timid, birds elusive, lions noble, asses silly—were utilized by visual satirists in their comment on the notables of the time. Goya's *Caprichos* are among the most enduring of the artistic associations of the bestial and human, but a lower form of this visual metaphor is frequently found in political satire. It is an easy solution to one of the most vexing problems faced by the cartoonist: identification of the subject of the drawing.

In his newspaper drawings, Oliphant has hardly ever used this form of visual metaphor, but lately he has returned to painting and has even branched out into sculpture as an extension of his visual conceptualization. Like one of his nineteenth-century idols, Honoré Daumier, who sometimes turned to sculpture as a means of creating figures that would later populate his lithographs or made sculptured figures based on characters that he had initially drawn, Oliphant has recently sculpted several of the presidents he had observed in office, and on occasion he has put them into association with animals. The evocative portrayal of Lyndon Johnson as a centaur—half horse, half man—is one of the most successful of these new works.

The artists of the sixteenth and seventeenth centuries were often strongly attracted by the expressive possibilities of physical deformity. Jacques Callot's capering dwarfs and grotesque beggars are justly celebrated, prefiguring the appearance of dwarf courtiers in the work of Velasquez. Leonardo da Vinci, P. L. Ghezzi, and other Italian painters reveled in the violent exaggeration of facial forms that were far from the Renaissance ideal of human beauty. One may question, however, whether these artists associated political or moral deformity with physical deformity, even when such identifiable characters as cardinals and clerics were depicted. Once in a while the association was inescapable, as in Erhard Schoen's portrayal of Martin Luther as—literally—the instrument of the devil. William Feaver described that woodcut as possibly "the first instance of an actual likeness used in print," but for the most part caricature was the private activity of the artist, undertaken for the amusement of his circle.

Caricature emerged as a public art around the time of King George III in England, when artists such as Thomas Rowlandson began to sell etched, hand-colored prints satirizing the behavior of public figures of the day, and commenting on the fashions, social customs, and political issues they introduced into a nation with an emerging urban middle class. As the rebellious behavior of some of the American colonists became more troublesome, the political tone of these etched cartoons became more strident, and soon book- and print-sellers found themselves deluged with published cartoons from many hands. A similar development occurred in France towards the end of the eighteenth century, as well as in other European centers.

Half a century or so after the American Revolution, and with the emergence of the illustrated periodical, artists were commissioned to prepare weekly or daily satiric drawings for public consumption. The challenge was to find a visual equivalent for a contemporary political or social issue that would clearly express the cartoonist's (or the editor's) outlook while it evoked the public personalities as vividly and unmistakably as possible. Early political cartoonists confronted these tasks in different ways and with varying degrees of effectiveness.

A rare genius such as Daumier could animate the people he drew with such brilliance, costume them so convincingly, and locate them in a scene with such authority that the comic possibilities of their condition could often be described with a minimum of text—often an exchange of dialogue between two of the people in the cartoon—printed below the drawing. Less-accomplished artists, especially in Great Britain and the United States, depended more on lengthy captions than on the eloquence of drawing to communicate their message to the reader. By the end of the nineteenth century a cartoon in *Punch* might be accompanied by a paragraph of prose, making the drawing little more than a scene-setting device for a playlet. This is usually not Oliphant's way. Occasionally the caption supplies the dialogue uttered by one of the characters in the drawing, but more often a few words suffice for him, as they did for Daumier, to underscore for the viewer what he is being invited to consider. The primary message is sent through the eloquent animation of the characters in the drawing, and through the rendition of the features of the recognizable principals.

Early on, the more imaginative comic artists realized that verbal and visual comment were distinct and different arts, and sought for fundamentally visual modes of satire. Some discovered that their audiences were sufficiently familiar with classical mythology or biblical stories to permit the transformation of contemporary confrontations into other, older contexts—often with highly amusing results. Daumier's translations of mid-nineteenth-century French social issues into scenes from ancient Greece (with the Parisian bourgeois protagonists uncomfortably clad in togas and sandals), FCG's (Francis Carruthers Gould) *Bird-Snaring in Hampshire*, which depicts 1903 British politics in a fifteenth-century woodcut style, or Thomas Nast's Tammany Tiger and reform lamb lying down together are but three examples from hundreds that might be cited. Oliphant uses this device infrequently, but when he does the analogies are equally telling. He referred to the fable of the grasshopper and the ant at one point in the Carter presidency, to be sure, but otherwise the Bible or Aesop are rarely utilized. On the other hand, President Reagan's former career afforded Oliphant with abundant opportunity to deal with a more modern source of characters and fables as he commented upon Reagan's frequent transformation of everyday realities into the context of the movies.

Oliphant has always been scornful of the artist who has to resort to using a label on the arm or coat of a character to notify the viewer that such-and-such a president or general is being portrayed. Today, through photographs, movies, and television, the faces of notables tend to be familiar, but in previous generations there was probably less likelihood that readers of newspapers in Chicago would recognize the French prime minister. It is always useful to have a dictator with a "signature" moustache (such as Hitler or Stalin), or a president who is very tall (Lincoln) or endowed with a prominent jaw (FDR). Otherwise, the caricaturist may be in difficulty. Even today, some occupants of high office have faces so lacking in eccentricity that the political cartoonist is hard-put to make them distinguishable—Oliphant dealt with Dan Quayle by making him faceless.

The cartoonist of genius often solves this by associating his characters with some attribute that speaks to the artist's view of his personality. Oliphant had no difficulty invoking President Carter through his toothy smile and abundant hair. As his political stature shrank, Carter's height in Oliphant's drawings also grew shorter and shorter. George Bush's lack of *machismo* was established by equipping him with a handbag, if not an entire woman's wardrobe.

One quality shared by caricaturists through the ages is the delight in swift, sure drawing. Rarely are visual satires highly finished drawings in the traditional sense, even though much labor may go into the distillation of the character being represented. Immediacy, not reflection, must be transmitted to the viewer; the liveliness (or lack thereof) of the subject must be expressed with an economy of line and shape. A few artists seem to have been given this gift in special abundance. Max Beerbohm had a special eye for gesture and placement. William Auerbach-Levy was unequalled in his ability to reduce a face to its most telling contour. Miguel Covarrubias was able to depict the incandescence of his jazz-age contemporaries while he reduced their features to a minimum of components.

Although few who have commented on his work have dwelt on this quality, I believe that Oliphant can be accorded a place in the pantheon of caricaturists. This is not to minimize the brilliance of his writing, the eloquence of the settings in which he places his characters, or the ingenuity with which he invokes metaphors for the issues upon which he comments. The reason he can dispense with labels for his principal characters is that he has drawn them with exceptional clarity and conciseness. It is a special privilege to be admitted behind the scenes of Oliphant's workroom and to see in his sketchbooks how, for example, the face of Reagan evolves from a straightforward portrait drawing, with features and hair style in normal proportions, into the Reagan of the published drawings, with an elongated upper lip, cheekbones ascending toward the eyes, and a rampant pompadour.

When the social satires of Thomas Rowlandson and James Gillray burst upon the British public in the eighteenth and early nineteenth centuries, etching was the medium of choice. Their hand-colored sheets communicated splendidly the artist's energetic and direct drawing, as did the lithographs of Daumier and his contemporaries. In both etching and lithography, the artist worked directly on the printing plate, and these media offered little interference to a fluently drawn line. This, however, was technically difficult to maintain in newssheets printed on the letterpress. Here, the drawing had to be reproduced through wood engraving, with the intervention of a professional engraver who translated the artist's fluid draughtsmanship onto a rigid woodblock. While the wiry and complex drawings of an artist such as Thomas Nast could stand up to this treatment, more delicate work lost its character altogether. Not until the perfection of photoengraving towards the end of the nineteenth century could artists hope for a more reliable translation of their drawings into published pictures, and even today most reproduced cartoons—fine as they are—cannot entirely capture the subtle variations of pressure and direction that the viewer senses when seeing an original drawing.

The exhibition that is the occasion for this book makes possible a full appreciation of the artistry with which Pat Oliphant has endowed his running commentary on the American presidency. From sketches (in which the presidential visage is transmuted from what nature provided to what Oliphant wants the viewer to see), through the drawings, which are finished in a morning for delivery to waiting messengers and impatient editors, to sculpture, which offers reflective distillations of the figure's most telling posture or eloquent gesture, we see an extraordinary display of portraiture, as well as of political comment. Those of us who are not the targets of Oliphant's scrutiny must be thankful that we have such a versatile artist in our midst and hope that we can look forward to at least another quarter-century of comment from his pen and brush.

ALAN FERN
Director
National Portrait Gallery

OLIPHANT'S PRESIDENTS:
Twenty-five Years of Caricature

Emerging from a cartoonist's daily labor to summarize, satirize, and explain current events and cultural trends are influential portraits of national leaders. In the course of twenty-five years in America, Australian-born artist Pat Oliphant has covered six presidents, from Lyndon Johnson to George Bush. His prize-winning, popular cartoons are syndicated to five hundred newspapers around the country and abroad. In this selection from the many thousands of drawings he has produced, the aim is not only to celebrate his twenty-five-year contribution to our political culture, but also to see him in a new light: as an artist whose remarkable skill at caricature has deepened our understanding of recent presidents and the modern presidency.

A political cartoonist, like any journalist, both reflects and influences public opinion about a prominent figure, but the portrait that emerges from successive cartoons is often subtle and cumulative as the artist repeats, sharpens, and modifies the caricature. The full impact of the portrayal is not always evident. Our usual response to a contemporary political cartoon is an assessment of how forcefully or cleverly the artist has summarized newsworthy issues or events of the day. To be effective, the central concept of the cartoon must dominate; and the composition must be simplified and focused to emphasize this idea. Often the famous people portrayed by the cartoonist are so familiar that their depiction registers less than the analogous situation in which they have been placed. The cartoon is "about" the Arab-Israeli peace talks or the Iran-contra scandal rather than Henry Kissinger or George Bush. So it is frequently not the portrayal of an individual in today's paper that influences us so much as the gradual building up over time, image by image, layer by layer, of a memorable characterization of that leader's strengths and weaknesses.

In the analysis of these cartoons as popular portraiture, all the elements that make a cartoon effective come into play. The first ingredient that secures a cartoonist's caricature in the public consciousness is a basic, repeated figural depiction that is at once distinctive, well drawn, humorous, and recognizable. Oliphant's distortions of a figure, particularly in the honeymoon of a presidency, tend to be subtle, avoiding broadly exaggerated or abstracted features. The addition of symbolic details, however, is often direct and forceful. How do intelligent leaders develop a reputation of being dumb? How do strong, athletic, virile men become perceived as bumbling, weak, or unmasculine? Surely a cartoonist's permanent bandaid on the president's forehead or ever-present lady's handbag on the arm are as much an influence as TV coverage of a fall on the ski slope or journalists' discussions of the "wimp" issue.

The other major ingredient that enriches the portrayal of an individual is the analogous imagery in the cartoon. With the insight and detachment of a foreign-born observer of American ways, Oliphant borrows inventively from the rich imagery of popular culture. Evoking Popeye or Theodore Roosevelt, conjuring up notions of the American cowboy hero or Hollywood movie star, taking advantage of emotional responses to sexual roles, surrogate motherhood, or homelessness, he adds layers of meaning and humor. His culturally weighted imagery has the advantage of being obvious and accessible, and, at the same time, complex and richly suggestive of shared, indigenous history, traditions, and emotions. The viewer's psychological and subconscious response to this imagery adds a crucial dimension to Oliphant's presidential caricatures.

Although the basic figural depiction is often repeated, there is nothing static about these caricatures; they gradually evolve and change, molding and reacting to public perceptions. Oliphant's presidents all start out relatively strong. In achieving our highest political office, a new chief executive has staged a spectacular electoral success. The winning rhetoric of the campaign and the patriotic music of the inaugural are still ringing in our ears. In the cartoons, the physical depiction as well as the analogous imagery generally portray a new president as grown-up, powerful, and masculine (although the latter quality does not apply to Bush, as will be discussed later). Although the cartoons are satiric and funny, images of cowboy, doctor, woodsman, athlete, or ship captain suggest physical strength and authority. As each president confronts complex domestic and international problems and inevitably fails to live up to our unrealistically high expectations, the physical distortions begin to change. Figures and faces bloat and sag, grow weak, small, or skinny. Instead of analogies of power or heroism, we see imagery of weakness, insanity, diminution, or corruption in a March Hare, a Mad Hatter, an ant, or a pirate.

In order to analyze fully Oliphant's presidential images, his well-known cartoons are supplemented here with less public depictions. These include bronze sculpture, lithography, color drawings for a poster, a book cover, and a magazine cartoon, and his remarkable, quick, insightful pencil sketches. In Oliphant's unpublished work, he is free from the constraints of a necessarily accessible, standardized, popular art form. Although he deploys the cartoonist's wit, analytical skills, and keen eye for caricature, he can explore more universal themes from mythology and western art, and add a focused aesthetic expression to his interpretations. The subtleties of his likenesses are often more discernible when they are not dominated by the theme of the cartoon. These works not only expand our appreciation of him as an artist, but they also help explicate the power and meaning of his cartoon portraits which have been so influential in the past quarter-century.

LYNDON JOHNSON

Oliphant's early images of Lyndon Johnson connote strength and control despite the satiric comment. In *Public Support* (1), the President is tough, lean, and armed in the best frontier tradition. The cowboy image, an inevitable analogy for the first Texan president, was too rich a theme in American popular culture to ignore, especially for an Australian newly arrived in Denver. The twentieth-century version of cowboy myth, popularized by pulp fiction, Western films, and TV serials, forged a potent national symbol. The image is not generally associated with leadership, but the qualities of physical strength, courage, independence, hard working resourcefulness, unsophisticated honesty, and innate sense of justice are traditional American character traits often sought in a president. In the imagery of Western dress and swinging saloon doors, these attributes are grafted onto the politician to create a particularly strong, indigenous concept of leadership.

The pending shootout in this cartoon refers to growing criticism of the quickly escalating Vietnam War. But the real subject is Johnson's acute pain at losing his public support after winning the greatest popular victory in American history in his 1964 election over Barry Goldwater. Public approbation was a deep-seated psychological need for Johnson, and here it is depicted as his young

'DO NOT FORSAKE ME, OH, MAH DARLIN'..!'

1. **Public Support**
A year after President John Kennedy's assassination, Lyndon Johnson regained the presidency with the greatest popular victory in American history. As the Vietnam War began to escalate, however, the public support he treasured so highly started to erode.

21

2. Popeye
Following surgery in 1966, Johnson resumed work on the ambitious legislative agenda of the Great Society with all his legendary energy.

'ALL RIGHT! OK! WE ALL KNOW YOU'RE FIT AND WELL!'

lover, to whom he clings in a rather unmanly way. Despite that weakness, it is apparent that Johnson will ultimately prevail. Not only does he have the positive attributes of a cowboy hero, but he also dominates because he is the only figure not drawn in the flat, abbreviated style of an animated cartoon or comic strip figure. Instead of round circles for eyes and a slit for a mouth, his features are fully drawn, just exaggerated.

In *Popeye* (2), LBJ himself becomes a comic strip hero as he rebounds from surgery in 1966. Popeye was the comic icon of strength, and LBJ's legendary

3. Night Reading
Johnson habitually spent hours every evening reading memos and reports from his staff. Here, the embattled President takes a break from his pressing problems to contemplate the birth of his first grandchild.

NIGHT READING

energy often seemed to defy any but mythic comparisons. So remarkable were his ambitious legislative agenda and his capacity for hard work that one aide credited him with having "extra glands." Despite the implication of unreasonable zeal, Popeye's power is an apt allusion to the muscular speed with which Johnson forced his Great Society programs through Congress.

Oliphant's depiction of Johnson had changed drastically by June 1967, when *Night Reading* (3) was published. The president of legendary strength is careworn, hunched over with exhaustion. Johnson was famous for his nighttime consumption of staff reports; here, he has set aside his reading on problems of the day—crime, the Middle East, Vietnam, and race riots—to await the arrival of his first grandchild. Alone, surrounded by darkness, and beset with problems, he is a very human figure, and a far cry from cowboy and cartoon heroes.

As *Night Reading* suggests, the generalized contours and abstracted features often used in animation and comic strip figures virtually disappeared from Oliphant's drawing at an early stage. Although cartoon characters can add an appealing charm or a note of crucial ridiculousness to the situation depicted, they did not fit with Oliphant's style or personality. Neither charm nor silliness have been a feature of his cartoons; his drawing is not sweet and his humor is not juvenile. Punk the penguin and his fellow observers, for instance, while very amusing, are a highly sophisticated tool for creating layers of meaning and humor. Kept small so as not to detract from the important central concept, these cynical bystanders variously add puns, regional accents, atmosphere, or even an extra prong to the attack. In *Night Reading*, Punk points out that the famous child care author, Benjamin Spock, was active in anti-war protests, adding poignancy to the beleaguered president's lonely vigil.

'YES, GENERAL WESTMORELAND, WE'RE WORKING ON YOUR QUOTA – HELLO DETROIT, HOW MANY HUNDRED THOUSAND TROOPS? – HOLD IT, THERE – HELLO, MINNEAPOLIS? . . .'

4. **Frazzled**
By the summer of 1967, Lyndon Johnson seemed to be losing control as General William Westmoreland demanded more troops in Vietnam and race riots flared up in Newark, Detroit, and Minneapolis.

5. The Six Faces of LBJ
A master of persuasion and arm twisting, Johnson could swagger, preach, or threaten as the situation demanded. Here, he performs as FDR, Don Quixote, and the devil himself in the pursuit of his goals, which ultimately required a much needed but greatly resisted tax increase.

In *The Six Faces of LBJ* (5), Oliphant probes Johnson's maverick and unpredictable style of leadership that made his power so effective. The President's persuasive skills on Capitol Hill had been hewn over a long career as congressman, senator, and majority leader. The cartoon refers to the large repertoire of effects he used in his highly personal approach to generating support for his agenda. In this masterful exercise in caricature, all the figures look like Johnson; but the puffed-up stance of the general is the essence of military arrogance, the downward glance of the priest is the summation of righteous piety, and the forward-leaning posture of the policeman is the epitome of threatening obtrusion. The price of the war and the programs that Johnson demanded or begged for, however, was a tax increase, and when he ran out of other roles, he could be the devil himself in manipulating legislators.

Johnson's dramatic and persuasive performances had little effect on the North Vietnamese nor could they stem the pent-up racial violence that exploded during his administration. These problems took their toll, as the cartoons *Frazzled* (4) and *Neutral Ship in a Neutral Sea* (7) clearly show. The strong leader has completely lost control. The taut lines of the cowboy and the massive bulk of the night reader have changed to a loose, baggy contour. Lines in the face, circles under the eyes, and the cleft in the chin have deepened. As one exploratory sketch makes clear, the sharp nose has grown bulbous and almost touches the protruding chin (11). In *Frazzled*, the President's propensity for using the telephone has turned into a nightmare: the lines are burning with crises, demands, and bad news, and Johnson cannot concentrate on anything. Worse, in *Neutral Ship in a Neutral Sea*, this frenetic and active man is completely still, helpless.

24

'DAMMIT! DOESN'T **ANYBODY** RECOGNIZE ME?'

6. The Great Reformer
Sincerely wishing to better the lives of his countrymen, and proud of the major legislation that already had been passed on civil rights and social programs, LBJ could not understand why protesting Americans did not recognize him as the greatest president since Abraham Lincoln.

'. . . AND FOR A NEUTRAL SHIP, NORTH KOREA HAS OFFERED THE PUEBLO!'

7. Neutral Ship in a Neutral Sea
Stalemated on finding a "neutral" site for the Vietnam peace talks, LBJ was also frustrated by protracted negotiations for the release of the USS *Pueblo*, which had been seized by North Korea in January 1968.

LBJ never understood why he was not appreciated for the remarkable amount of civil rights and social welfare legislation he shepherded through Congress. Sincere in his vision of progress, he could not see the Vietnam War eclipsing his Great Society legacy. In the image of Johnson as Lincoln in *The Great Reformer* (6), the depth of his frustration and his delusion are apparent. With his gnarled hand clutching a shawl and his weak legs tucked around the

8. Retirees
Johnson's announcement on March 31 that he would not seek his party's nomination in 1968 was a political bombshell. French president Charles De Gaulle, facing problems of his own, here also contemplates retirement.

"'AH WILL NOT SEEK, NOR WILL AH ACCEPT . . .' HOW DID THAT GO AGAIN?"

9. Benched
The Senate's humiliating rejection of Abe Fortas, LBJ's nominee for chief justice, was symptomatic of the sidelining of a president who had once been a major player in the Democratic Party, the Congress, and the White House.

rocking chair, he looks old and wizened, but this is not a pitiful or sympathetic portrayal of age. The growling dog and Punk's comment of "Sic 'im" reflect the extent of public hostility towards the President.

The cartoon *Benched* (9), of October 1968, shows how completely Johnson had lost his touch. From unprecedented power in Congress and an unprecedented presidential victory at the polls to a complete loss of influence was a devastating journey. Abe Fortas, Johnson's nominee for chief justice, had just

'NOW HERE'S A LITTLE PROBLEM I'VE SET UP FOR YOU TO SOLVE ALL BY YOURSELF!'

10. **Driving Lesson**
After several years of simultaneously funding the Great Society and the Vietnam War, the United States economy was in trouble. A few months before the 1968 election, Johnson finally pushed through a surtax, leaving the political and economic ramifications for Richard Nixon, the successor he so bitterly opposed.

been rejected by the Senate, a humiliating defeat for a president who was once the undisputed master of that body. Johnson's stock in the Democratic Party was so low that he did not even attend the presidential convention. More than just breaking his bat, he has forgotten how to play the game.

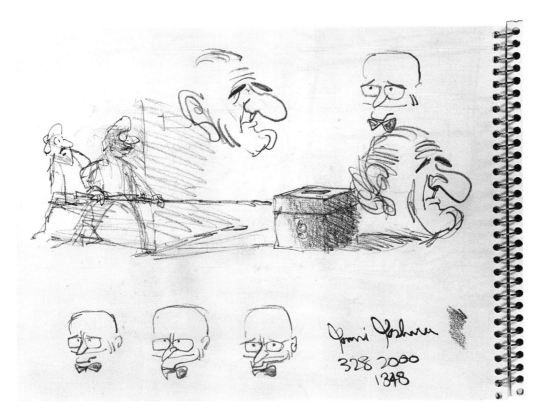

11. Two heads of LBJ and other sketches

13. Lyndon Johnson
(Color plate p. 65)

In *Retirees* (8), Oliphant returns to the cowboy image. Back in his boots and Stetson, LBJ has left the stifling atmosphere of Washington for the great, wide spaces. Less romantic is his exit from "Surtax Gulch" in *Driving Lesson* (10). With the cowboy's resourcefulness in the face of danger, he slips away, leaving his successor to deal with the unpopular new tax. In these cartoons, there is a sense of relief that Johnson has finally relinquished his enormous power. Yet once safely away from Washington, he is allowed to be the aging cowboy of waning strength who fades gracefully away.

Oliphant used the cowboy imagery again in cartoons of other presidents. In his sculpture, however, he explored the subject of man and horse more deeply, merging ancient traditions of classical mythology and equestrian portraiture with the indigenous American cowboy theme. His bronze *Lyndon Johnson* (13), a centaur wearing a Western hat, focuses on the mythic element of this enigmatic and unusual man who was so often described in hyperbolic terms. Since the centaur was attributed with the strength of a horse but was wild, licentious, and unpredictable, the sculpture suggests Johnson's independence from the historical summarizing, categorizing, and stereotyping that is often the fate of presidents.

RICHARD NIXON

The evolution of Richard Nixon is, predictably, the most dramatic of any of Oliphant's presidents. In early images of his presidency, Nixon is a suave political maneuverer. His heavy eyebrows and side-glancing eyes suggest a certain slyness as he forces the anti-ballistic missile down the taxpayer's throat in *Now, Swallow Hard* (14). As opposed to the brutal military advisor behind him, Nixon's role is that of a doctor prescribing the proper remedy—labeled "℞ Taxpayer ABM"—and helpfully offering a glass of water to ease the discomfort. The image connotes superior knowledge and unchallengeable authority despite the heavy-handed tactics.

There is no question who is responsible for the administration's Vietnam policies in *Low Profile?* (15). In this cartoon, Nixon not only controls military strategy by personally disgorging bombs, but he also manipulates public opinion by flashing peace signs, projecting a low profile, and discussing "protective reaction." A cool precision and a similar sense of authority prevails as he locks the door on *The Nixon Cabinet* (16), constraining his appointed officials. Requiring no explanation, the cartoon's central idea is simple and very apt; the President's approach to governing is neatly summarized in one dominating image of arrogance and control.

'NOW, SWALLOW HARD!'

14. Now, Swallow Hard
Nixon lobbied intensively for the controversial anti-ballistic missile (ABM), one of his early legislative priorities. One obstacle was the unsympathetic Senator Margaret Chase Smith, whose contradictory votes on the amendments baffled most observers.

15. Low Profile?
Nixon's Vietnam policy included both the withdrawal of U.S. troops and the resumption of bombing. Since White House rhetoric was sometimes used to disguise unpopular actions, the public was often confused by developments in the war.

16. The Nixon Cabinet
Nixon believed in keeping tight control over his cabinet officials.

'. . . AND THAT IS WHY WE CALL IT A CABINET.'

While most of Oliphant's presidents grow old and lose authority and stature, a more powerful transformation affects his caricatures of Nixon. As the Watergate scandal begins to unfold, Nixon is changed into a searing image of evil. His face sags and bloats, turning into a truly grotesque and hideous parody of the earlier slick politician. At first a haunted paranoia developed. In *Watergate Bug* (17), he skulks in a dark corner, peering out with terror in his eyes. In *Security Blanket* (18), irrational, child-like fear dominates, and the blanket and thumb are the childish defenses against the mysterious terrors of the night.

'DO YOU THINK IT'S STILL HUNGRY . . ?'

SECURITY BLANKET

By the time of Nixon's resignation, the caricatured figure had become the essence of hardened corruption. In the cartoon *Shopping for a Special Prosecutor* (19), Nixon is portrayed as a pirate, an image of lifelong criminality where brutal and rapacious force is the only measure of dominance. The President had finally succeeded in firing special prosecutor Archibald Cox, although both the attorney general and his deputy resigned in protest. The cartoon summarizes Nixon's hope that he can find a "pet" prosecutor who will listen to instructions. It portrays not only an action but also a mental attitude towards the problems the President was facing.

19. Shopping for a Special Prosecutor
Having finally succeeded in firing special prosecutor Archibald Cox, a desperate Nixon hoped for the appointment of a successor whom he could control.

'I NEED A NICE POLITE PARROT WHO'LL SIT ON MY SHOULDER AND SPEAK WHEN HE'S SPOKEN TO!'

20. Ask Me Anything
Off-stage, fangs bared, Nixon asks Press Secretary Ron Ziegler to add more names to the White House "enemies list," revealing his conviction that politics was less of a game than it was all-out war.

'I WANT A LIST OF THE NAMES OF ALL THOSE WHO ASKED EMBARRASSING QUESTIONS!'

The essential characteristics of the caricatures in Oliphant's work can be better understood by examining his pencil sketches. These deft, rapid drawings are mostly preliminary versions of cartoon ideas. In addition to working out his basic concept, he sometimes experiments with exaggerations of the face (see 11). Most important for this study, the sketches often convey the caricature portrait in its most elemental form before the composition has been edited and focused to bring out the primacy of the central cartoon idea. With a single exception (69), the sketches are not paired here with finished drawings but are used on

'I WISH I COULD SHARE YOUR OPTIMISM, JIM, BUT TO ME IT ALL LOOKS RATHER HOPELESS—THE NFL WILL NEVER SETTLE THIS STRIKE BY FALL!'

21. The Pessimist
Oblivious to his pending downfall, Nixon discusses football with presidential defense counsel James St. Clair a month before his resignation.

'JERRY, ABOUT YOUR PROPOSED UPPER-INCOME SURTAX . . . WILL THAT APPLY TO MY $55,000 PENSION, OR MY $200,000 TRANSITION ALLOWANCE?'

22. Nixon in Retirement
Nixon, here nursing a painful attack of phlebitis, retired to his San Clemente estate, but his seemingly luxurious lifestyle angered many who resented his presidential pardon.

their own to expand the viewer's understanding of the caricature image as it is first captured on paper. For instance, in the tiny sketch of Nixon as a vulture sitting on Reagan's shoulder (25), the face of the latter is loosely sketched and barely recognizable. In contrast, the bird's head is an exquisite and careful study of evil. The final cartoon refers to Nixon's suggestion of Alexander Haig as secretary of state. The face of the vulture has to compete with the more finished portrait of Reagan and with our feelings about the absent subject, Al Haig. It is

33

23. **Looking for Trees**
In this cartoon about Nixon's generous transition allowance, a bloated and corrupt image of the former president is contrasted with the figure of Ford as a myopic but simple and sturdy woodsman.

LOOKING FOR TREES

24. Six heads of Nixon preparing for a TV show

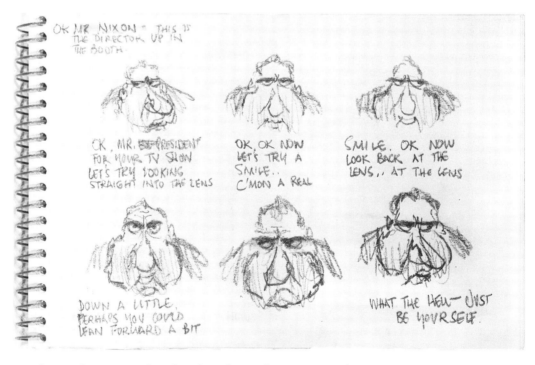

in the preliminary sketch, therefore, that we can best understand Oliphant's powerful concept of what the image of Nixon had come to mean.

Another important theme in the post-retirement images of Nixon is the public's enduring sense of outrage towards the man who had betrayed its trust. As depicted in *Nixon in Retirement* (22), the ex-president, now pardoned and living on a California estate, is a grotesquely distorted figure. The cartoon refers to his generous transition allowances, yet it says more about what a hateful,

25. Nixon as vulture on Reagan's shoulder

26. Head and bust of Nixon

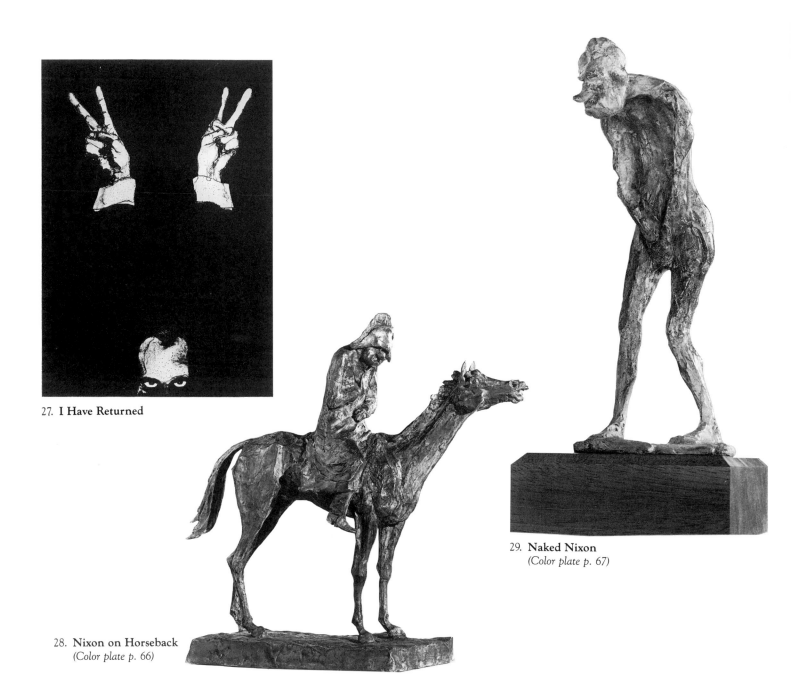

27. **I Have Returned**

28. **Nixon on Horseback**
(*Color plate p. 66*)

29. **Naked Nixon**
(*Color plate p. 67*)

festering irritant he had become for the American public. He left office, but he refused to disappear. The print *I Have Returned* (27), which utilizes the full power of a rich black lithographic tone, evokes the dark, unsettling feelings many experienced during Nixon's occasional forays back into public life. The sculpture of Nixon as Napoleon (28) is a new twist on the equestrian leader tradition, suggesting a malevolent presence that keeps returning to haunt us. The depth of feeling about Nixon is expressed with raw power in the small figure of the bronze *Naked Nixon* (29). Even so many years after Watergate, it touches a nerve. It does not seem quite funny the way a naked President Bush (81) would. Perhaps the public's tortured embarrassment and sense of violation, as well as Nixon's, are portrayed here.

GERALD FORD

From the start it was clear that Gerald Ford would offer neither the drama nor the trauma of Nixon's presidency. Nevertheless, Oliphant scrutinized the President, his actions, and his evolving image just as seriously on a day-to-day basis. In *Looking for Trees* (23), Ford is depicted as a woodsman. Searching for spending cuts, he misses the biggest tree of all—Nixon's incredible transition allowances. Despite his myopia, the muscular strength and simplicity of the woodsman image suggest a return to solid American morals and values. The lack of a sophisticated political veneer was welcome. Less innocent is the inky black, looming figure in *Biting the Bullet* (32), but Ford's massive bulk connotes power and strength, particularly in contrast to the small, weak taxpayer.

Americans have always projected moral superiority and an indigenous sort of courage onto their athletic heroes, and sports analogies seemed particularly apt for the new president with his sturdy physique and clean-cut image. In *Going Swimming* (31), Ford is in the pool, ready to go the distance to lower inflation. Knowing that he would need the help of long-time Nixon foe George Meany, Ford invited the combative president of the AFL-CIO over for an informal chat in the Oval Office. In contrast to a hilariously grotesque Meany, who seems reluctant to even test the waters, Ford appears as an experienced swimmer. In a

30. Waiting Room
The day before Nixon's resignation, Gerald Ford waits to assume the presidency and contemplates the new potential in the old political rallying cry, "Bring Us Together."

31. Going Swimming
Trying to promote an "open" White House, Ford invited AFL-CIO president George Meany over for a chat soon after taking office. Ford no doubt hoped to enlist the union boss' good will in the coming battle against inflation.

GOING SWIMMING

32. Biting the Bullet
In his battle against record-high inflation and unemployment, Ford seemed to have a clear preference for defense spending over social programs.

'NOW, BITE ON THE BULLET—THAT'LL STOP YOU WASTING ALL YOUR MONEY ON FOOD!'

less-flattering cartoon about relations with Israel (33), Ford is being battered, but at least he is in there fighting. Although he is draped pathetically on the ropes, he is still a massive figure.

As Ford's presidency continued, however, the sturdy simplicity that seemed comforting in the woodsman becomes simplemindedness in the statesman. In *Low Wattage* (34), Oliphant lampoons his incompetence in foreign affairs, his dependence on Henry Kissinger, and the impotence of Congress with a changing-

'I THINK WE CAN GET A RETURN BOUT WITH ISRAEL, IF THAT HELPS...'

33. **A Return Bout?**
Ford felt somewhat battered by Israel's hard-line intransigence after Henry Kissinger's Middle East negotiations broke down in March 1975.

'YOU CONGRESS TYPES ARE SO DAMN SMART WITH THIS FOREIGN POLICY STUFF—HELP HENRY TURN THE LADDER!'

34. **Low Wattage**
Since the President was perceived as having had minimal experience with foreign policy, Secretary of State Kissinger is shown playing a pivotal role, with Congress as a mere spectator.

the-light-bulb, "dumb" joke. The insult to all of them is emphasized in the caption, "You Congress types are so damn smart with this foreign policy stuff—help Henry turn the ladder!" The congressmen, shoved in a pack to one side, are weak figures depicted in tones of gray. Completely left out of the decision-making process, they do not even seem capable of the demeaning role the President has suggested for them. Their ineptness does not make Ford seem

35. **Economic Advisors**
With inflation and unemployment high, and the stock market and GNP low, the economy was a menacing problem in 1975. Ford's solutions seemed primitive and his economic advisors about as effective as a bunch of baboons.

'SO, FINE, HE'S GOING TO GET TIRED... WHEN IS HE GOING TO GET TIRED??'

36. **Hammered Head**
In a futile, last-ditch attempt to postpone South Vietnam's final capitulation, Ford asked Congress for $722 million in emergency military aid in April 1975. Congress refused.

'WHY? BECAUSE IT'S GOING TO FEEL SO GREAT WHEN I QUIT... THAT'S WHY!'

stronger; instead it only reinforces the impression of complete incompetence in setting foreign policy.

In *Economic Advisors* (35), Ford's economists as well as his solutions to menacing economic problems are forcefully depicted as primitive, if not sub-human. The President's Tarzan image is a parody of strength, only serving to prove that brute muscularity is useless if not supported by intelligence. And the adult Ford is completely dominated by Kissinger, who is portrayed as a bratty and spoiled child in *A Kick in the Shins* (37). As he stands precariously on one

40

"I HAVE BEEN ADVISED THAT THIS STATEMENT IS PROBABLY INCORRECT..."

foot with a pained expression on his face, Ford is clearly a defeated figure. In contrast to the bickering is campaign manager Rogers Morton's deadpan explanation as he removes his glasses in a dry, professorial manner. As so often happens in Oliphant's cartoons, the caption adds just the right tone and accent to emphasize the personality: "I have been advised that this statement is probably incorrect. . . ." It is a perfect evocation of the obfuscating statements issued by spokesmen to cover for White House squabbles.

Just as Ford's intellectual strength began to decline in the cartoons, so did his physical stature. Bandaids began to appear in Oliphant's images of Ford,

39. Performer and Critic
The one critic who should have been sympathetic to Jimmy Carter's meager early performance as president was the predecessor who had struggled with the same insoluble problems.

40. Bust of Ford with bandaids

signaling the serious questioning of the President's overall coordination and competence that emerged after a series of televised stumbles, trips, and falls. As the President headed for defeat at the polls after two short years in office, the greatly diminished cartoon images help to explain why. In *Pardon Me* (38), a pencil sketch (40), and a sculpted mask (42), Ford's elongated, ape-like face, with its banal smile, vacant eyes, and bandaids, is a reminder of how completely he had lost public confidence.

42. **Gerald Ford**
   (*Color plate p. 68*)

JIMMY CARTER

In the wake of Vietnam, Watergate, and severe economic problems, a crisis of confidence deeply affected relationships between the presidency and the press, the Congress, and the public. Jimmy Carter was able to capitalize on this loss of respect towards authority when he defeated the incumbent and won the 1976 election as a Washington outsider, but skeptical attitudes towards the executive office would bedevil him throughout his presidency. In Oliphant's early images of Carter, a corny campaign smile dominates the figure. The disarming charm of that down home, country grin seemed to be all that people noticed in their search for new leadership. Reasons to stop smiling are clearly outlined, however, in an inauguration day cartoon (43) as Carter inherits the difficult problems his predecessor had faced. The rumpled clothes, celebratory streamer, and automatic smile are a neat summary of the campaigner. Tellingly, the rest of his face is obscured. What intelligence, character, and leadership qualities lay behind the smile?

The firm moral values of a born-again Christian was one quality people did recognize in Carter, although it was as often a liability as it was an asset outside the Bible Belt. In Oliphant's cartoons, it was a frequent theme. The

"GOOD MORNING, MR. PRESIDENT... AND YOU CAN STOP SMILING NOW!"

43. Stop Smiling
When Jimmy Carter took office as a relatively untested national politician, he inherited difficult issues that were guaranteed to wipe the ever-present campaign smile off his face.

44. Fence Mending
Pushing unpopular farm and water policies, Carter found fence mending difficult on an October 1977 trip to several Western and Midwestern states that he had lost in the election.

THE FENCES HAVE BEEN MENDED ON THE WEST FORTY

45. Businessmen's Lunch
Carter never gained the confidence of business leaders, and his emphasis on minor abuses, such as the deductible three-martini lunch, suggested puritanical niggling more than strong leadership or an inspiring moral tone.

BUSINESSMEN'S LUNCH

sanctimonious face of Carter defying Congress on sanctions to Zimbabwe-Rhodesia in *The Missionary* (47) suggests stubborn and arrogant righteousness rather than strong moral leadership. The no-nonsense puritan waitress (45) taking orders in "Mother Karter's Karrot Kitchen Kafe" is similarly inflexible in her ban on three-martini lunches. As so often is true in Oliphant's work, the central concept of Carter-as-puritan is layered with more subtle touches of meaning. Punk's comment of "Gimme a Co'Cola shooter!—hang th' expense" adds a touch

RAFSHOON
ASSOCIATES

PATCHWORK
PUBLIC
RELATIONS

IMAGES WORKED
OVER

SUBSTANCE
& FORM
REVISED

THE NEW
ME!

TA-DAH

46. The New Me
With the help of communications assistant Gerald Rafshoon, Carter made a largely futile midterm attempt to strengthen his image.

ZIMBABWE-RHODESIA
SANCTIONS

SHUSH! MASSA CARTER KNOWS WHAT'S RIGHT FOR YOU!

THE MISSIONARY

47. The Missionary
Carter, a born-again Christian, here preaches his own vision as he defies Congress and refuses to lift trade sanctions against Zimbabwe-Rhodesia.

of Southern redneck to the New England puritan for a particularly narrow-minded combination. The negative tone of the signs on the wall—"no spirituous liquors," "no dancing," "no smoking either"—not only adds to the humor but also suggests the nature of the whole relationship between Carter and the business world. The President never did gain the confidence of financial leaders. His righteous objections to deductible expenses certainly did not inspire better business ethics, nor did his sour relationship with the world of finance help his economic programs.

48. The Goddam Ant
Cast here as a busy little working ant versus Senator Ted Kennedy's frivolous grasshopper, Carter shrinks into insignificance in a presidential role crafted by his press secretary, Jody Powell.

'AW, JEEZ, JODY, DO I HAVE TO BE THE ANT? I MEAN, I UNDERSTAND THE MOTIVES OF THE PLAY, BUT PLAYING A GODDAM ANT...??'

49. Scuba Driver
Carter struggled to receive the 1980 nomination from a Democratic Party that often seemed to be completely controlled by Ted Kennedy, despite questions about the senator's car accident at Chappaquidick, which involved the drowning death of a female passenger. This drawing was made for the cover of the 1980 book *Oliphant: A Cartoon Collection* and is inscribed to Texas-born playwright Larry L. King, who wrote the foreword.
(Color plate p. 69)

Sensitive to his falling popularity in the polls, Carter attempted to improve his public image of leadership in 1978 with the help of communications assistant Gerald Rafshoon. Despite the efforts and promises of public relations packaging ("Substance & Form Revised"), *The New Me* (46) is only an inflated clone of the old Carter. As the new image is built up, the original is diminished. In a devastating transformation in subsequent cartoons, Oliphant's Carter simply shrinks in size in relation to advisors, opponents, and international leaders.

UNIVERSAL PRESS SYNDICATE
©1980 WASHINGTON STAR
OLIPHANT

ELECTION STRATEGY

THINK OF IT AS
A BRIEFING,
ED!

STATE

'...AND I THINK IT WOULD BE NICE IF WE COULD NUKE IRAN OR FREE POLAND
SOMETIME IN OCTOBER...'

50. Election Strategy
Advisors Harold Brown, Robert Strauss, Zbigniew Brzezinski, and Edmund Muskie react to Carter's global strategies for winning the 1980 election.

THE PEACE OFFICER

KEEP YOUR EYES
PEELED FOR
WARMONGERS

51. The Peace Officer
As the election approached, Carter seemed increasingly incompetent at solving international crises, particularly in the Middle East, where war had just broken out between Iran and Iraq.

Carter plays an earnest but ridiculously tiny ant in contrast to Ted Kennedy's oggling grasshopper in Oliphant's version of Aesop's fable (48). The script, written and directed by influential press secretary Jody Powell, is meant to portray Carter as hard working, but instead he seems only insignificant and sure to be upstaged by Kennedy. The most poignant element of the cartoon, however, is Carter's self-conscious realization of his diminishing powers of leadership. "Aw, jeez, Jody," he complains. "Do I **have** to be the **ant**? I mean, I

52. **Your Ship, Captain**
The public lack of confidence in the presidency was at a particularly low ebb when Carter turned the ship of state over to one who seemed to promise much more.

understand the motives of the play, but playing a goddam **ant**. . . ??" The clear recognition of his own failings (a quality so lacking in his successor) as well as the sincerity of his attempts to improve are expressed with humorous intensity.

Carter's backseat position to Ted Kennedy required neither quote nor caption in *Scuba Driver* (49), a cartoon redrawn in color for the cover of an Oliphant book. The brushstrokes of the car imply speed and motion, as does Kennedy's braced but confident position at the wheel. Carter's hilarious expression of discomfort suggests both his certainty of pending disaster and his utter powerlessness. The same painful awareness is evident in the small sketch (55) of Carter unable to sell his memoirs because of the presence of the giant "killer" rabbit that had purportedly attacked him on a fishing trip. "You're not helping, you know," he remarks dolefully to the animal.

The international failures of the Carter presidency—the hostage crisis, the Iran-Iraq war, OPEC's collusion on oil prices, the invasion of Afghanistan—seemed all the more disappointing and frustrating to the public after the high expectations set by the Camp David accords between Israel and Egypt. Carter's impotence in solving these problems reinforced the image of shrinking stature and power. The sketch of Carter standing in the hand of Khomeini and asking for his endorsement (54) suggests not only Carter's insignificance but also the enormity of the Ayatollah's psychological power over Americans during the hostage crisis. As a nation, we seemed to be held in the palm of his hand. Carter sits on top of the globe, trying to create an international event that might help his candidacy, in *Election Strategy* (50). He has not grown any larger; his world has simply grown smaller. In *The Peace Officer* (51), Carter has lost all ability to grapple with foreign crises. He even lacks his self-awareness as he ambles obliviously through the destruction.

53. Carter Aid [Carter with bandaid]

54. Carter standing in Khomeini's hand

Like many of his other presidential sculptures, Oliphant's bronze of Carter (57), is a summation of the cartoon images. As he perches on a corner, legs dangling over the side, the abstract setting makes his miniaturization all the more forceful. He is morose and sullen, but the tragedy of his personal failures has shrunk along with his figure. He has become too insignificant to elicit great sympathy.

55. Carter and the Killer Rabbit

57. **Jimmy Carter**
(Color plate p. 70)

56. Full length of Carter

RONALD REAGAN

Confidence in the presidency was at a particularly low ebb when Carter lost the election to Ronald Reagan in 1980 (52). The new president seemed a grander man with greater promise. In his 1976 cartoon *The Cardboard Messiah* (58), Oliphant begins to develop the movieland theme that he used with great effect in images of Reagan. The genial figure is larger than life, a "giant replica of a statesman." Implied is not only the exaggerated hype of Hollywood promotion, but also the shallowness and fragility of the cardboard cutout and the movie set, constructed for pure dramatic effect and lacking foundations or real purpose. Nonetheless, like the closeup on the movie screen, the size of the figure makes Reagan—and his promises—seem super real rather than unbelievable. His audience is not a group of skeptical voters but adoring, uncritical fans.

58. The Cardboard Messiah Narrowly losing the Republican nomination to Gerald Ford in 1976, former actor Ronald Reagan already seemed larger than life to some and shallower than a movie set cardboard cutout to others.

Oliphant continued to explore the theme of the presidency as Hollywood fiction in *Standing Tall* (60). Here, the sentimental rhetoric of Reagan's promises to make America proud again is compared with the simplistic quality of good-versus-evil movie fantasy. Reagan is cast as a Hollywood character type, the military hero. The implication of the traditional image is power, impressive physical stature, moral superiority, courage, and cool decision-making at a time

UNIVERSAL PRESS SYNDICATE
©1981 WASHINGTON STAR

59. Hold Real Still, Sam
Shortly after his inauguration, Reagan is shown promising a keen aim and a tough stance in dealing with pesky trouble-makers, such as Cuban president Fidel Castro, who was supplying arms to leftist guerillas in El Salvador.

'HOLD REAL STILL, SAM... I'LL JUST KNOCK THE ASH OFF HIS CIGAR.'

60. Standing Tall
With the simplicity of Hollywood heroism, Reagan attempts to prove American superiority on the island of Grenada and elsewhere. The reclaimed heroine looks askance at his heavy-handed tactics.

of crisis. Yet America, the rescued victim, seems appalled by some of the hero's notions: the evil empire of Andropov, the greed of the phantom hungry, the threat of tiny Grenada. She clearly possesses a more sophisticated understanding of complex domestic and international problems.

The invasion of Grenada is the subject of Oliphant's small sketch of Reagan as Teddy Roosevelt (68), a predecessor of unquestioned patriotism and great physical strength and courage. The humor of the drawing comes from the fact that Roosevelt's imperialistic notions of might are several generations out of date, and, the public, like Reagan, had little idea of Grenada's place in the

THE SILENCED MAJORITY

'CUT!'

international arena or why American forces had landed there.

Despite the suggestions of shallowness and simplicity, these early images depict Reagan as gigantic and powerful. In *Hold Real Still, Sam* (59), he is an armed cowboy, aged to be sure, but still with a steady hand and complete confidence in hitting his target. Disposing of Fidel Castro, who had been supplying arms to leftist guerillas in Latin America, is mere child's play in this context. And despite the obvious threat of catastrophe, only Punk seems nervous; Uncle Sam appears to be more worried about the hornet.

63. I'm after Communists!
In his single-minded assault on Communism in Latin America, Reagan ignores the underlying problems of countries such as Nicaragua.

64. Golly, What a Story!
Reagan translates the inspiring news of Jeana Yeager and Dick Rutan's round-the-world non-stop flight into such sentimental drivel and personal aggrandizement that even his wife cannot bear it.

Inevitably, the image of vigor eroded as the Reagan presidency began to lose momentum. Reagan's face became longer, blanker, more age-worn, and perplexed. In *The Silenced Majority* (61), the head appears to be completely empty, a hollow vessel to be filled with the opinions of influential advisors. The only conscious decision this Reagan seems capable of making is which ear to cork. A mildly alarmed president longs for the simple omniscience of movie making in *Cut* (62). Apparently not quite bright enough to panic, he seems a perfect parody of the resourcefulness of the American cowboy ideal.

65. Frankly, No
Denying knowledge of details of the Iran-contra arms-for-hostages deal, Reagan appears to be losing control over his government, while powerful forces such as the Soviet Union's Gorbachev, South Africa's Botha, Iran's Khomeini, and a speculative stock market are strengthening their grips on international events.

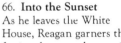

66. Into the Sunset
As he leaves the White House, Reagan garners the affection due a cowboy savior at the sunset fadeout and seems to believe fully the film-fantasy version of his role as statesman.

"He likes to keep things simple," Punk tells an observer in *I'm after Communists!* (63), where Reagan ignores disease, poverty, ignorance, and war in his search for Communists in Nicaragua. A comparison with the initial pencil sketch (69) shows how Oliphant simplified and sharpened his composition in the finished pen and ink cartoon, taking out a horseman, a child, and the woman's pointing finger. The ominous threat of the horsemen is heightened in the ink drawing by the contrasts of shadowy black and sunbaked white, while the turned head of Reagan's horse connects the two groups, suggesting that the beast sees

67. Wonderland
Reacting to the problems of Attorney General Edwin Meese, the President appears as ingenuous as the Mad Hatter, his wife Nancy as vicious as the Queen of Hearts, and Vice-President Bush as vacantly alert as the March Hare controlled by a higher command.

68. Reagan as Teddy Roosevelt arriving on Grenada

'NO, THAT'S NOT THE GANG I'M LOOKING FOR, MA'AM — I'M LOOKING FOR COMMUNISTS'

what Reagan cannot. Yet even in the quick preliminary sketch, the figure of Reagan is established. With his back to the real criminals, he leans slightly towards the pregnant woman, tips his hat, and speaks politely. His kindly, gentle manner towards her adds tragic irony to the depiction of a cruelly oblivious and narrow-minded policy.

The perception of Reagan as being out of touch with the decision-making process in his administration was greatly heightened by the Iran-contra scandal. Claiming ignorance of the exact details of the arms-for-hostages deal made Reagan appear to have lost control. In *Frankly, No* (65), the rumpled clothes, wrinkled face, intertwined fingers, and hesitant speech—"Do you ever feel that maybe things have . . . gotten away from you?"—combine to give an impression of advanced senility. The weakness of his lightly sketched figure contrasts with the bulky, thick, black masses of Gorbachev, Botha, Khomeini, and the stock exchange. Their strength, intransigence, arrogance, and irresponsibility, as well as their increasing control over events, are implied. Once equal to them, Reagan seems to have abdicated his power.

From here it is a short step to the depiction of Reagan as a Mad Hatter (67). *Wonderland*, a term first applied to the Justice Department, is depicted as an "all-pervasive atmosphere." The Queen of Hearts (Nancy Reagan) and the March Hare (George Bush) are just as mad as the hatter; and the viewer, reacting much like Alice, is both amused and amazed by the administration's strange and thoroughly illogical world.

Oliphant returned to the movie theme in a retirement cartoon of Reagan (66). The cowboy hero galloping into the sunset is such a familiar image that one

70. Reagan as scarecrow,
heads of Ortega and Reagan

71. Bust of Reagan

73. **Reagan on Horseback**
(Color plate p. 71)

can almost hear the sentimental music that accompanies it. The President and
his wife, entirely recognizable from the back, are completely taken in by this
hackneyed but well-loved cliché ending. They cannot separate the glowing movie
version of Reagan's accomplishments from reality. Neither can the American

public, is the implicit suggestion. Part of its enduring affection for Reagan may be the public's need for a simplified, Hollywood presidential hero, who never seeks a compromise or admits a mistake—a cowboy sheriff to go after the bad guys.

In his sculpture of Reagan on horseback (73), Oliphant once again added a new dimension to the cowboy-president, equestrian-leader theme. He implies that to Reagan, the presidency was a wildly exhilarating ride on a bucking broncho—for as long as he could hold on. The expectation that this rider will soon be unseated contrasts with the solid, monumental permanence depicted in most equestrian statuary. Despite his exuberance, Reagan's loss of control over his frantically gyrating steed gives a slightly sickening sense of imminent disaster.

COLOR PLATES

13. Lyndon Johnson

28. **Nixon on Horseback**

29. **Naked Nixon**

42. **Gerald Ford**

49. **Scuba Driver**

57. **Jimmy Carter**

73. **Reagan on Horseback**

83. Altered Egos

84. From George to George

90. George Bush

GEORGE BUSH

In comparison to Reagan, George Bush did not seem a promising subject for brilliant cartoon humor. He was not as old or as new, not as conservative or as sentimental, and he had never been a movie actor. At the beginning of Bush's presidency, however, Oliphant had already probed beyond the blandness to find amusing and revealing themes. Early in the campaign, he started to explore questions of class and notions of strength and weakness as they pertained to masculinity. When Bush announced his candidacy in the fall of 1987, he promised to be a real tiger. In Oliphant's cartoon (74), he is every bit as ferocious as a kid in a costume. No one, especially the conservative "daughters of ye Reagan Revolution," is fooled. The tea party setting here is critical, establishing Bush's East Coast, moneyed, aristocratic background as a key factor in his persona and his presidency. There is a stiff-upper-lip lack of political emotion and commitment implied in this cartoon—"My goodness, how very thrilling, George . . . one lump or two?"—as well as the absence of a virile and manly ability to fight.

In *Altered Egos* (83), the image of Bush that "they try to sell" is the strong, courageous, young fighter pilot. What is perceived, however, is a delicate Southern

GEORGE BUSH DECLARES FOR 1988: "YOU'RE GONNA SEE A REAL TIGER OUT THERE!" HE SAID.

74. A Real Tiger
Hoping to inherit Reagan's supporters in his presidential bid, George Bush promises to be a ferocious campaigner, but conservatives are only mildly impressed.

debutante. The lack of masculine toughness is subsequently summarized in many campaign cartoons, with the repetition of a symbolic purse on the candidate's arm (75). When the purse is combined with one of our most enduring concepts of American masculinity, the Texas cowboy image (76), the symbol resonates with the sexual confusion of our generation. The unraveling of strict masculine and feminine stereotypes is implied here as well as our desperate groping for sexual roles and identity. The cartoon is funny without being threatening because Bush is not effeminate, only too finely bred to seem very masculine. His attempt to claim a masculine cowboy image is marvelously ludicrous.

The feminine image that has the most emotional resonance is the small sketch of George Bush as a surrogate mother (85). The concept of surrogacy is a brilliantly witty analogy to his denial, as vice-president, of responsibility in the

'WOW! GOLLY, SO IT IS! WELL, GOSH, IT'S BEEN YEARS! AND HOW ARE THINGS WITH YOU, DAD?'

77. Dad
Candidate Bush's assertion that he was an environmentalist sounded hollow after eight years as vice-president in a determinedly anti-environment administration.

' I ADORE THE BUSH STYLE, BUT I THINK IT LOOKS BETTER ON BARBARA.'

78. The Bush Style
The newly elected president undoubtedly wished he was as popular as his wife Barbara, whose warm, caring personality and homey, non-threatening image had endeared her to the American public. She had just been the subject of a complimentary cover story in *Time* magazine.

Iran-contra affair. The shape and stance of the figure is wonderfully reminiscent of pregnancy, yet more is at stake here in our reaction to the depiction of a newly declared candidate for the presidency. Surrogate motherhood was a hotly debated subject at the time. The emotions it aroused were based on deep, instinctual fears of infertility, parental rejection, baby buying, and even genetic selection. No matter how funny the image, the emotional intensity of this issue hovers in the background and raises to a new level the implicit questions of Bush's moral and ethical relationship to the scandal and to his denial of responsibility.

'OH, THE HECK WITH IT — I'D RATHER BE THE EDUCATION PRESIDENT.'

Not only does Bush seem to lack manly strength, but so does the entire elite, Ivy League, WASP power structure for which he stands. As political power begins to pass out of the hands of the traditional "old boy" establishment, Bush appears to be the last of a breed. In a speech to unemployed steelworkers, Bush describes a kinder and gentler America (87) where "everyone owns a squash racket, where everybody's daughter has a coming-out party." He clearly represents an upper-class establishment that is essentially out of touch with mainstream America.

THE EMPEROR DISPLAYS HIS NEW WARDROBE.

81. **The Emperor's New Clothes**
Several months into his presidency, Bush seemed to have nothing to show the public but bare campaign promises.

82. **People's Puppy Program**
White House enthusiasm over the arrival of a litter of First Puppies supplanted other priorities that demanded the President's attention, such as drugs and crime.

A particularly strong indictment is the cartoon *Dad* (77), which refers to candidate Bush's rediscovery of the environment after eight years of neglect as vice-president. The huddled image of the homeless man also suggests the cuts in social welfare programs during the Reagan-Bush administration. In contrast to the hunched image of misery is the upright figure of a conservatively dressed Bush, who looks like a Wall Street investment banker. His ingenuous surprise and polite inquiries are startling and horrifying, invoking the yuppie moral degeneracy of Tom Wolfe's *Bonfire of the Vanities*. The point of the cartoon is Bush's stand on environmental issues, but these powerful images also suggest that he represents a segment of society that is no longer fit to govern.

83. **Altered Egos**
Bush's campaign image as a
heroic World War II navy pilot is contrasted with a bland,
Southern belle weakling;
Michael Dukakis' sturdy immigrant figure shrinks to a mi-
nute and insignificant average
person.
(Color plate p. 72)

Bush's physical characteristics in Oliphant's work underscore this process of decline. In some of the early campaign images, such as the sketch of a squabbling Bush and Senator Robert Dole sitting on Reagan's lap (86), the Vice-President is small and juvenile, too young to assume the role of his parent. Gradually, however, as he approaches the presidency, he grows up and becomes increasingly elongated and emaciated. In the attenuated forms of *Dad* and the sculpture of Bush throwing horseshoes (90), he seems weak, pampered, overbred, and overrefined. He has sat too long in the boardroom, too little in the saddle; he appears the opposite of the sturdy immigrant stock of his 1988 opponent, Michael Dukakis (83). Indeed, he is the end of a declining breed. The naked president wearing nothing but a purse and empty hangers in *The Emperor's New Clothes* (81) is an amusing parody of that strong masculine ideal to which an American patriarchal president is supposed to conform.

80

84. **From George to George**
This poster was commissioned by the National Trust for Historic Preservation in celebration of the bicentennial of the presidential inaugural. The printed version, entitled *Celebrating America's Main Street*, also commemorated the role of historic preservation in the restoration of Pennsylvania Avenue. Bush lived up to his poster image by walking down the avenue during the inaugural parade.
(Color plate p. 73)

    Ironically, Barbara Bush conveyed that strength of character Americans want to see in their president. Shortly after a flattering cover story about her appeared in *Time* magazine, Oliphant published his cartoon *The Bush Style* (78). The President, looking absurd (as does Punk) in white-haired drag, is not only envious of her appeal, but he is also overly eager to conform to popular taste, whatever it may be. In attempting to ape Barbara's style and confidence in herself, of course, he further undermines his own.

85. Bush as surrogate mother

86. Bush and Dole as children on Reagan's lap

It is not George Bush's actual physical prowess that is lampooned, but the strength of his leadership. These images are much funnier and not as vicious as the Civil War cartoons of Jefferson Davis wearing petticoats; they do not carry the personal emasculating message of an earlier era. They do, however, place the

87. Bush speaking to
steelworkers

GUYS,
'I SEE A KINDER, GENTLER AMERICA, WHERE EVERYONE OWNS A SQUASH RACKET,
WHERE EVERYBODYS DAUGHTER HAS A COMING-OUT PARTY, THERE ARE NO LIBERALS...'
WHERE

88. Bush and Congress in
honeymoon bed

AHEM

CONGRESS

LET THE HONEYMOON COMMENCE,

president firmly within the context of our changing sexual and ethnic consciousness. These feminine images negate outdated equations that masculinity equals
power and suggest the imminence of a more inclusive political atmosphere. In
laughing at the weakness of the man, we sense the fragility of the traditional
white male power structure.

Because popular art forms are directed to a wide audience rather than to a specialized elite, their images and references must be easily understood. If the overt meanings of Oliphant's cartoons are obvious, however, the underlying significance is often subtle and complex, drawing upon deep-seated psychological responses and cultural traditions. Oliphant's sophisticated use of layers of shared understanding has particular importance in his portrayal of individuals. As the physical depiction of each president gradually changes, it is given poignancy and power through the meaning of the imagery, the humor of the witty punch line, and the enhancement of Punk's colorful observations. The combination of these elements creates a vivid statement about the individual. Since the cartoon often focuses attention on the issue or event, the portrayal is a subtle one that gradually develops a powerful message over time. By looking beyond his daily cartoons to sculpture and other media, we can more fully understand Oliphant's interpretations of these individuals.

Frequently Oliphant manages to scratch some personal itch arising from our own frustration with governmental leaders. But some of the enormous satisfaction we derive from his cartoons can be explained by his ability to go beyond the specific to elucidate the general trends in our national life. Remarkably attune to the nuances of American traditions, he defines the cultural context in which each president has succeeded and in which he has inevitably failed. Against this rich background, Pat Oliphant creates his popular portraiture, reinterpreting those familiar features with dazzling wit and original insight.

84

AUTHOR'S NOTES

The exhibition of *Oliphant's Presidents* originated at the National Portrait Gallery and was toured by Art Services International. In addition to the staffs of these two institutions and the lenders mentioned above, I am indebted to Susan Conway Carroll, who launched and coordinated this endeavor from the start, handling infinite details for both author and artist. I am particularly grateful for the inspiration and cooperation of Pat Oliphant, who produced more presidential sculpture for the exhibition, created titles for the cartoon drawings that lacked them, pulled pieces from storage, and provided generous encouragement and assistance throughout the project.

WENDY WICK REAVES
Curator of Prints and Drawings
National Portrait Gallery
Smithsonian Institution

CHECKLIST

Dimensions are given in inches and centimeters; height precedes width precedes depth.

LYNDON JOHNSON

Cartoons

1. Public Support
Caption: *'Do not forsake me, oh, mah darlin'. . !'*
Cowboy to Punk: *Hah newn* **already**—*how time flies!*
India ink over pencil on duoshade artist's board, July 12, 1965
11¹⁵/₁₆ x 17¹/₂ (30.3 x 44.5)
Western Historical Collections, University of Colorado, Boulder

2. Popeye
Caption: *'All right! OK! We all know you're fit and well!'*
Punk: *Barbequed spinach* **again?**
Hubert Humphrey: *With* **tapioca!**
India ink over pencil on duoshade artist's board, November 22, 1966
11³/₄ x 17⁹/₁₆ (29.9 x 44.7)
Western Historical Collections, University of Colorado, Boulder

3. Night Reading
Caption: *Night reading*
Punk: *Isn't Dr. Spock in the peace moveme. . .?*
Aide: **Shaddup!**
India ink over pencil on duoshade artist's board, June 21, 1967
11¹/₈ x 17⁵/₈ (28.3 x 44.8)
Western Historical Collections, University of Colorado, Boulder

4. Frazzled
Caption: *'Yes, General Westmoreland, we're working on your quota—Hello Detroit, how many hundred thousand troops?—Hold it, there—Hello, Minneapolis? . . .'*
Punk: *Watt?*
India ink over pencil on duoshade artist's board, July 24, 1967
11⁵/₈ x 17⁹/₁₆ (29.6 x 44.7)
Western Historical Collections, University of Colorado, Boulder

5. The Six Faces of LBJ
Caption: *'However . . !'*
India ink over pencil on duoshade artist's board, January 19, 1968
11⁵/₈ x 17⁹/₁₆ (29.5 x 44.7)
Western Historical Collections, University of Colorado, Boulder

6. The Great Reformer
Caption: *'Dammit! Doesn't <u>anybody</u> recognize me?'*
Punk: *Sic 'im!*
India ink over pencil on duoshade artist's board, February 13, 1968
12¹/₈ x 17⁹/₁₆ (30.9 x 44.7)
Western Historical Collections, University of Colorado, Boulder

7. Neutral Ship in a Neutral Sea
Caption: *'. . . And for a neutral ship, North Korea has offered the Pueblo!'*
Punk: *Just be certain you're a long ways* **off-shore!**
India ink over pencil on duoshade artist's board, May 2, 1968
11⁷/₈ x 17⁹/₁₆ (30.2 x 44.7)
Pat Oliphant, Courtesy of Susan Conway Carroll Gallery

8. Retirees
Caption: *" 'Ah will not seek, now will Ah accept . . .' How did that go again?"*
Punk: *Git ol' Chuck a copy of the text, Tex!*
India ink over pencil on duoshade artist's board, May 26, 1968
12¹/₁₆ x 17⁹/₁₆ (30.6 x 44.7)
Pat Oliphant, Courtesy of Susan Conway Carroll Gallery

9. Benched
Punk: *Odd game!*
Observer: *Odd country!*
Observer: *. . . But loveable*
India ink over pencil on duoshade artist's board, October 2, 1968
11¹³/₁₆ x 17⁵/₈ (30 x 44.8)
Western Historical Collections, University of Colorado, Boulder

10. **Driving Lesson**
Caption: *'Now here's a little problem I've set up for you to solve all by yourself!'*
Punk: *Which way to Recessionsville?*
Mountaineer: *Straight down!*
India ink over pencil on duoshade artist's board, November 19, 1968
12⁵/₁₆ x 17¹/₂ (31.4 x 44.5)
Western Historical Collections, University of Colorado, Boulder

Sketches

11. Two heads of LBJ and other sketches
Pencil on paper (sketchbook), 1984
6 x 8 (15.3 x 20.3)
Pat Oliphant, Courtesy of Susan Conway Carroll Gallery

12. Two sketches of LBJ as a centaur
Pencil on paper (page from sketchbook), 1984
6 x 8 (15.3 x 20.3)
Pat Oliphant, Courtesy of Susan Conway Carroll Gallery

Sculpture

13. **Lyndon Johnson**
Bronze, 1984
18 x 7¹/₂ x 14 (45.7 x 19.1 x 35.6)
Pat Oliphant, Courtesy of Susan Conway Carroll Gallery

RICHARD NIXON

Cartoons

14. **Now, Swallow Hard**
Caption: *'Now, swallow hard!'*
Punk: **Try** *to remember how you voted, Senator Chase Smith!*
India ink over pencil with opaque white on duoshade artist's board, August 8, 1969
11⁹/₁₆ x 17⁵/₈ (29.4 x 44.8)
Pat Oliphant, Courtesy of Susan Conway Carroll Gallery

15. **Low Profile?**
Caption: *Low profile?*
Punk: **Please!** *Don't call it bombing—call it protective reaction!*
India ink over pencil on duoshade artist's board, December 1, 1970
11¹/₂ x 17⁵/₈ (29.3 x 44.8)
Pat Oliphant, Courtesy of Susan Conway Carroll Gallery

16. **The Nixon Cabinet**
Caption: *'. . . And that is why we call it a cabinet.'*
Man to Punk: *Soundproof, too!*
India ink over pencil on duoshade artist's board, November 30, 1972
11¹/₂ x 17⁵/₈ (29.3 x 44.8)
Pat Oliphant, Courtesy of Susan Conway Carroll Gallery

17. **The Watergate Bug**
Caption: *'Do you think it's still hungry. . ?'*
Bug to Punk: *So much for the hors d'oeuvres!*
India ink over pencil on duoshade artist's board, 1973
11⁷/₁₆ x 17⁵/₈ (29.1 x 44.8)
Pat Oliphant, Courtesy of Susan Conway Carroll Gallery

18. **Security Blanket**
Caption: *Security blanket*
India ink over pencil on duoshade artist's board, May 30, 1973
12³/₁₆ x 17⁵/₈ (31 x 44.8)
Pat Oliphant, Courtesy of Susan Conway Carroll Gallery

19. **Shopping for a Special Prosecutor**
Caption: *'I need a nice polite parrot who'll sit on my shoulder and speak when he's spoken to!'*
Punk: *You're needed up front!*
India ink over pencil on duoshade artist's board, October 30, 1973
11¹/₂ x 17⁹/₁₆ (29.3 x 44.7)
Pat Oliphant, Courtesy of Susan Conway Carroll Gallery

20. **Ask Me Anything**
Caption: *'I want a list of the names of all those who asked embarrassing questions!'*
Aide: *This is the President's offensive!*
Punk: *More and more offensive!*
India ink over pencil on duoshade artist's board, November 15, 1973
11¹/₂ x 17⁹/₁₆ (29.3 x 44.7)
Pat Oliphant, Courtesy of Susan Conway Carroll Gallery

21. **The Pessimist**
Caption: *'I wish I could share your optimism, Jim, but to me it all looks rather hopeless—the NFL will never settle this strike by fall!'*
Pat Nixon to Punk: *He was hoping to find work as a coach this year . . .*
India ink over pencil on duoshade artist's board, July 2, 1974
11½ x 17½ (29.3 x 44.6)
Pat Oliphant, Courtesy of Susan Conway Carroll Gallery

22. **Nixon in Retirement**
Caption: *'Jerry, about your proposed upper-income surtax . . . Will that apply to my $55,000 pension, or my $200,000 transition allowance?'*
Punk: *Call your tax lawyer*
India ink over pencil on duoshade artist's board, October 4, 1974
11⁹⁄₁₆ x 17⁹⁄₁₆ (29.3 x 44.6)
Pat Oliphant, Courtesy of Susan Conway Carroll Gallery

23. **Looking for Trees**
Caption: *Looking for trees*
Punk: *That's a bit of ecology we could do without!*
India ink over pencil with opaque white on duoshade artist's board, September 1, 1974
11⁹⁄₁₆ x 17⅝ (29.3 x 44.8)
Pat Oliphant, Courtesy of Susan Conway Carroll Gallery

Sketches

24. Six heads of Nixon preparing for a TV show
Pencil on paper (sketchbook), 1983
4 x 6 (10.1 x 15.2)
Pat Oliphant, Courtesy of Art Wood

25. Nixon as vulture on Reagan's shoulder
Pencil on paper (sketchbook), 1980
4 x 6 (10.1 x 15.2)
Pat Oliphant, Courtesy of Art Wood

26. Head and bust of Nixon
Pencil on paper (page from sketchbook), 1982
9 x 12 (22.8 x 30.5)
Pat Oliphant, Courtesy of Art Wood

Lithograph

27. **I Have Returned**
Lithograph, 1985
24 x 17¾ (60 x 45.1)
Pat Oliphant, Courtesy of Susan Conway Carroll Gallery

Sculpture

28. **Nixon on Horseback**
Bronze, 1985
17¾ x 19¾ x 5½ (45.1 x 50.2 x 14)
Pat Oliphant, Courtesy of Susan Conway Carroll Gallery

29. **Naked Nixon**
Bronze, 1985
7¾ x 3 x 2¾ (19.7 x 7.6 x 7)
Pat Oliphant, Courtesy of Susan Conway Carroll Gallery

GERALD FORD

Cartoons

30. **Waiting Room**
Punk: *You want to dust that off?*
India ink over pencil on duoshade artist's board, August 7, 1974
11½ x 17⁹⁄₁₆ (29.3 x 44.7)
Pat Oliphant, Courtesy of Susan Conway Carroll Gallery

31. **Going Swimming**
Caption: *Going swimming*
Punk: *Anyone who can get George in there can't be all bad!*
India ink over pencil on duoshade artist's board, August 16, 1974
11⁹⁄₁₆ x 17⁹⁄₁₆ (29.4 x 44.7)
Pat Oliphant, Courtesy of Susan Conway Carroll Gallery

32. **Biting the Bullet**
Caption: *'Now, bite on the bullet—that'll stop you wasting all your money on food!'*
Punk: *Trade unions and large corporations come forward and collect your bullets!*
India ink over pencil on duoshade artist's board, October 4, 1974
11½ x 17⁹⁄₁₆ (29.3 x 44.7)
Pat Oliphant, Courtesy of Susan Conway Carroll Gallery

33. A Return Bout?
Caption: *'I think we can get a return bout with Israel, if that helps . . .'*
Punk: *Maybe you should stay with golf!*
India ink over pencil on duoshade artist's board, 1975
11½ x 17⁹/₁₆ (29.3 x 44.7)
Pat Oliphant, Courtesy of Susan Conway Carroll Gallery

34. Low Wattage
Caption: *'You Congress types are so damn smart with this foreign policy stuff—help Henry turn the ladder!'*
Punk: *'Don't meddle,' he says . . .*
India ink over pencil on duoshade artist's board, February 16, 1975
11½ x 17½ (29.3 x 44.6)
Pat Oliphant, Courtesy of Susan Conway Carroll Gallery

35. Economic Advisors
Caption: *'So, fine, he's going to get tired . . .* **When is he going to get tired??'**
Punk: *You get what you pay for, Tarzan!*
India ink over pencil on duoshade artist's board, April 29, 1975
11½ x 17⁹/₁₆ (29.3 x 44.7)
Pat Oliphant, Courtesy of Susan Conway Carroll Gallery

36. Hammered Head
Caption: *'Why? Because it's going to feel so great when I quit . . . That's why!'*
Congressman to Punk: *He gives me a headache*
India ink over pencil on duoshade artist's board, 1975
11⁹/₁₆ x 17⁹/₁₆ (29.4 x 44.7)
Pat Oliphant, Courtesy of Susan Conway Carroll Gallery

37. A Kick in the Shins
Caption: *"I have been advised that this statement is probably incorrect . . ."*
Ron Nessen to Punk: *First Bo Calloway, now,* **this***!*
India ink over pencil on duoshade artist's board, April 6, 1976
11½ x 17⁹/₁₆ (29.2 x 44.7)
Pat Oliphant, Courtesy of Susan Conway Carroll Gallery

38. Pardon Me
Punk: *. . . And the alternative is Jimmy the Peanut*
India ink over pencil on duoshade artist's board, October 6, 1976
11⁹/₁₆ x 17⁵/₈ (29.4 x 44.8)
Pat Oliphant, Courtesy of Susan Conway Carroll Gallery

39. Performer and Critic
Musician to Punk: *Jerry played so well, you know*
India ink over pencil on duoshade artist's board, April 22, 1977
11⁹/₁₆ x 17⁹/₁₆ (29.4 x 44.7)
Pat Oliphant, Courtesy of Susan Conway Carroll Gallery

Sketches

40. Bust of Ford with bandaids
Pencil on paper (page from sketchbook), 1982
9 x 12 (22.8 x 30.5)
Pat Oliphant, Courtesy of Art Wood

41. Mask of Gerald Ford
Pencil on paper (page from sketchbook), 1989
8 x 6 (20.3 x 15.2)
Pat Oliphant, Courtesy of Susan Conway Carroll Gallery

Sculpture

42. Gerald Ford
Bronze, 1989
10 x 6¼ x 5¼ (25.4 x 15.9 x 13.3)
Pat Oliphant, Courtesy of Susan Conway Carroll Gallery

JIMMY CARTER

Cartoons

43. Stop Smiling
Caption: *"Good morning, Mr. President . . . and you can stop smiling now!"*
Punk: *Party's over, Jimmy!*
India ink over pencil on duoshade artist's board, January 20, 1977
11½ x 17⁵/₈ (29.3 x 44.8)
Pat Oliphant, Courtesy of Susan Conway Carroll Gallery

44. Fence Mending
Caption: *The fences have been mended on the west forty*
India ink over pencil on duoshade artist's board, October 25, 1977
11⁵/₈ x 17⁹/₁₆ (29.6 x 44.7)
Pat Oliphant, Courtesy of Susan Conway Carroll Gallery

45. **Businessmen's Lunch**
Caption: *Businessmen's lunch*
Punk: *Gimme a Co'Cola shooter!—hang th' expense*
India ink over pencil on duoshade artist's board,
December 17, 1977
11½ x 17⁹/₁₆ (29.3 x 44.7)
Pat Oliphant, Courtesy of Susan Conway Carroll
Gallery

46. **The New Me**
Punk: *Ta-dah*
India ink over pencil on duoshade artist's board,
1978
11½ x 17⁹/₁₆ (29.3 x 44.7)
Pat Oliphant, Courtesy of Susan Conway Carroll
Gallery

47. **The Missionary**
Caption: *The missionary*
Punk: *Shush! Massa Carter knows what's right for you!*
India ink over pencil with opaque white on duo-
shade artist's board, June 10, 1979
11³/₈ x 17¹/₈ (28.9 x 43.6)
Pat Oliphant, Courtesy of Susan Conway Carroll
Gallery

48. **The Goddam Ant**
Caption: *'Aw, jeez, Jody, do I **have** to be the **ant**? I mean, I understand the motives of the play, but playing a goddam **ant**. . . ??'*
Punk: *Type-cast again!*
India ink over pencil on duoshade artist's board,
May 10, 1979
11³/₈ x 17³/₁₆ (28.9 x 43.7)
Pat Oliphant, Courtesy of Susan Conway Carroll
Gallery

49. **Scuba Driver**
Punk: *Geronimo!*
India ink and colored inks on artist's board, 1980
12¹/₈ x 20¹/₁₆ (30.8 x 50.9)
Larry L. King and Barbara S. Blaine

50. **Election Strategy**
Caption: *'. . . And I think it would be nice if we could nuke Iran or free Poland sometime in October . . .'*
Punk: *Think of it as a briefing, Ed!*
India ink over pencil on duoshade artist's board,
August 28, 1980
11¹/₄ x 17¹/₄ (28.5 x 43.8)
Pat Oliphant, Courtesy of Susan Conway Carroll
Gallery

51. **The Peace Officer**
Caption: *The peace officer*
Punk: *Keep your eyes peeled for warmongers*
India ink over pencil on duoshade artist's board,
October 28, 1980
11³/₁₆ x 17¹/₄ (28.5 x 43.8)
Pat Oliphant, Courtesy of Susan Conway Carroll
Gallery

52. **Your Ship, Captain**
Caption: *'Your ship, Captain!'*
Punk: *I am bailing!*
India ink over pencil on duoshade artist's board,
January 20, 1981
11⁷/₁₆ x 16⁷/₈ (29.1 x 42.9)
Pat Oliphant, Courtesy of Susan Conway Carroll
Gallery

Sketches

53. Carter Aid [Carter with bandaid]
Pencil on paper (sketchbook), 1980
4 x 6 (10.1 x 15.2)
Pat Oliphant, Courtesy of Art Wood

54. Carter standing in Khomeini's hand
Caption: *Hi, I'm Jimmy Carter and I'm running for president. My opponent is a terribly dangerous war-monger and I therefore seek your endorsement*
Pencil on paper (sketchbook), 1980
4 x 6 (10.1 x 15.3)
Pat Oliphant, Courtesy of Art Wood

55. Carter and the Killer Rabbit
Caption: *'You're not helping, you know . . .'*
Pencil on paper (sketchbook), 1982
4 x 6 (10.2 x 15.3)
Pat Oliphant, Courtesy of Art Wood

56. Full length of Carter
Pencil on paper (page from sketchbook), 1982
9 x 12 (22.8 x 30.5)
Pat Oliphant, Courtesy of Art Wood

Sculpture

57. **Jimmy Carter**
Bronze, 1989
6³/₄ x 3³/₄ x 4¹/₄ (17.2 x 9.5 x 10.8)
Pat Oliphant, Courtesy of Susan Conway Carroll
Gallery

RONALD REAGAN

Cartoons

58. The Cardboard Messiah
Caption: *The Cardboard Messiah Starring Ronald Reagan as the Giant Replica of a Statesman*
Punk: *Another disaster movie?*
India ink over pencil on duoshade artist's board, January 9, 1976
11⁹/₁₆ x 17⁹/₁₆ (29.4 x 44.7)
Pat Oliphant, Courtesy of Susan Conway Carroll Gallery

59. Hold Real Still, Sam
Caption: *'Hold real still, Sam . . . I'll just knock the ash off his cigar.'*
Punk: *Let's do this in one take—OK?*
India ink over pencil with opaque white on duoshade artist's board, February 24, 1981
11⁷/₁₆ x 16⁷/₈ (29.1 x 42.9)
Pat Oliphant, Courtesy of Susan Conway Carroll Gallery

60. Standing Tall
Caption: *America's back and REAGAN'S got her! Scornful of the deficit dangers, he sent his marines to die in far-off lands for apple pie, for church and flag, for school prayer, for his political keister. Suddenly America was STANDING TALL (PG) . . . and cost was no obstacle!*
Punk: *Costarring the US Marines th[e . . .] the Pope Grenada. Euro[pe]*
Bugs Bunny to Punk: *Ehhh! (crunch) It's only a movie, Doc!*
India ink over pencil on artist's board, January 26, 1984
11¹/₈ x 17¹/₂ (28.4 x 44.5)
Pat Oliphant, Courtesy of Susan Conway Carroll Gallery

61. The Silenced Majority
Caption: *The silenced majority*
India ink over pencil on artist's board, July 29, 1983
11¹/₈ x 17³/₈ (28.4 x 44.2)
Pat Oliphant, Courtesy of Susan Conway Carroll Gallery

62. Cut!
Caption: *'Cut!'*
Punk and crew: *Lights! Camera! Teflon!*
India ink over pencil with opaque white on artist's board, June 25, 1985
11¹/₄ x 17¹/₂ (28.6 x 44.5)
Pat Oliphant, Courtesy of Susan Conway Carroll Gallery

63. I'm after Communists!
Caption: *'No, that's not the gang I'm looking for, ma'am—I'm after Communists!'*
Punk: *He likes to keep things simple*
India ink over pencil with opaque white on artist's board, March 17, 1986
11⁵/₁₆ x 17⁹/₁₆ (28.8 x 44.7)
Pat Oliphant, Courtesy of Susan Conway Carroll Gallery

64. Golly, What a Story!
Caption: *Golly, what a story! Two American pilots flying non-stop around the world! What strength of character, what straight guts and fortitude! Hey, it's what made this country great—truth, plain-dealing, integrity, light, honesty, honor, distinction— Why, it's everything I've lived for— It's the American way! It's my way!!*
Punk: *He's doing the best he can!*
India ink over pencil on artist's board, December 26, 1986
11⁹/₁₆ x 17¹/₂ (29.4 x 44.6)
Pat Oliphant, Courtesy of Susan Conway Carroll Gallery

65. Frankly, No
Caption: *Do you ever feel that maybe things have . . . gotten away from you?*
Punk: *I refuse to answer that . .*
India ink over pencil with opaque white on artist's board, January 9, 1987
11¹/₂ x 17⁹/₁₆ (29.2 x 44.7)
Pat Oliphant, Courtesy of Susan Conway Carroll Gallery

66. Into the Sunset
India ink over pencil with opaque white on artist's board, January 16, 1989
11¹/₂ x 17¹/₁₆ (29.3 x 43.3)
Raymond C. Weigel

67. Wonderland
Caption: *'Golly—how can they say that?'*
Punk: *Maybe it's the all-pervasive atmosphere*
India ink over pencil on artist's board, July 29, 1988
11 x 14 (28 x 35.7)
Pat Oliphant, Courtesy of Susan Conway Carroll Gallery

Sketches

68. Reagan as Teddy Roosevelt arriving on Grenada
Caption: *Bully! Where am I?*
Pencil on paper (sketchbook), 1983
8 x 10 (20.3 x 25.4)
Pat Oliphant, Courtesy of Art Wood

69. Reagan looking for Communists in Nicaragua
Caption: *'No, that's not the gang I'm looking for, ma'am—I'm looking for Communists*
Pencil on paper (sketchbook), 1986
4 x 6 (10.2 x 15.3)
Pat Oliphant, Courtesy of Susan Conway Carroll Gallery

70. Reagan as scarecrow, heads of Ortega and Reagan
Caption: *Embargo of Nicaragua*
Pencil on paper (sketchbook), 1985
9 x 12 (22.8 x 30.5)
Pat Oliphant, Courtesy of Susan Conway Carroll Gallery

71. Bust of Reagan
Pencil on paper (page from sketchbook), 1989
8 x 6 (20.3 x 15.2)
Pat Oliphant, Courtesy of Susan Conway Carroll Gallery

72. Reagan and buffalo in the White House
Caption: *A home where the buffalo roam.*
Pencil on paper (sketchbook), 1988
6 x 8 (15.3 x 20.3)
Pat Oliphant, Courtesy of Susan Conway Carroll Gallery

Sculpture

73. **Reagan on Horseback**
Bronze, 1985
12 x 10³/₄ x 11¹/₂ (30.5 x 27.3 x 29.2)
Pat Oliphant, Courtesy of Susan Conway Carroll Gallery

GEORGE BUSH

Cartoons

74. **A Real Tiger**
Caption: *George Bush declares for 1988: "You're gonna see a real tiger out there!" he said.*
Punk: *Pretty stirring*
Dog: *Yep*
India ink over pencil with opaque white on artist's board, October 13, 1987
11¹/₂ x 17¹/₂ (29.2 x 44.4)
Pat Oliphant, Courtesy of Susan Conway Carroll Gallery

75. **Sleeping Dog**
Punk: *Let sleeping dogs lie, like everyone else does*
India ink over pencil with opaque white on artist's board, March 15, 1988
11 x 13⁵/₈ (28 x 34.6)
Pat Oliphant, Courtesy of Susan Conway Carroll Gallery

76. **Boo-teek Texan**
Caption: *OK, George—fill yore hand, yo' boo-teek Texan!*
Punk: **Smile** *when you says thet, stranguh!*
India ink over pencil with opaque white on artist's board, July 13, 1988
11 x 14 (27.9 x 35.7)
Pat Oliphant, Courtesy of Susan Conway Carroll Gallery

77. **Dad**
Caption: *'Wow! Golly, so it* **is***! Well, gosh, it's been* **years***! And how* **are** *things with* **you***, Dad?'*
Observer to Punk: *Dad's out of the loop.*
India ink over pencil with opaque white on artist's board, September 14, 1988
11 x 14¹/₁₆ (27.9 x 35.7)
Pat Oliphant, Courtesy of Susan Conway Carroll Gallery

78. **The Bush Style**
Caption: *'I adore the Bush style, but I think it looks better on Barbara.'*
Punk: *Maybe we shoulda got Barbara for president*
India ink over pencil with opaque white on artist's board, January 24, 1989
11⁹/₁₆ x 17 (29.3 x 43.3)
Pat Oliphant, Courtesy of Susan Conway Carroll Gallery

79. **Mother and Child**
Caption: *My goodness, listen to that—little Danforth's first word in office!*
Punk: *You must be so proud*
India ink over pencil on artist's board, March 13, 1989
11¹/₂ x 17¹/₁₆ (29.3 x 43.4)
Pat Oliphant, Courtesy of Susan Conway Carroll Gallery

80. **The Environment President**
Caption: *'Oh, the heck with it—I'd rather be the education president.'*
India ink over pencil with opaque white on artist's board, April 6, 1989
11⁵/₈ x 17⁷/₁₆ (29.6 x 44.4)
Pat Oliphant, Courtesy of Susan Conway Carroll Gallery

81. The Emperor's New Clothes
Caption: *The emperor displays his new wardrobe.*
Punk: *You need a tie to go with that?*
India ink over pencil on artist's board, July 25, 1989
11½ x 17 (29.3 x 43.2)
Pat Oliphant, Courtesy of Susan Conway Carroll Gallery

82. People's Puppy Program
Caption: *Tsk! Drugs, guns, shooting, killing. What all those people need is a **puppy**!*
Advisor: *Another bold initiative—implement that!*
Punk: *'President proposes people's puppy program'?*
Advisor: *'Doggies for druggies'*
India ink over pencil with opaque white on artist's board, March 21, 1989
11½ x 17¹/₁₆ (29.3 x 43.3)
Pat Oliphant, Courtesy of Susan Conway Carroll Gallery

83. Altered Egos
Caption: *Bush: What they try to sell   As he is perceived*
Dukakis: What they try to sell   As he is perceived
Punk: *Or, how we think of them, when we think of them at all*
India ink and color pencils on vellum paper, September 1988 (*Regardie's* magazine)
14 x 11 (35.6 x 28)
Pat Oliphant, Courtesy of Susan Conway Carroll Gallery

Poster

84. From George to George
Punk: *Beautiful, ain't it, George? Er George?*
India ink, colored inks, colored pencils, and airbrushed acrylic, with opaque white on artist's board, 1989
30 x 26¼ (76.2 x 66.8)
National Trust for Historic Preservation

Sketches

85. Bush as surrogate mother
Caption: *'It belongs to Mr. Reagan—I'm just a surrogate.'*
Pencil on paper (sketchbook), 1987
4 x 6 (10.2 x 15.2)
Pat Oliphant, Courtesy of Susan Conway Carroll Gallery

86. Bush and Dole as children on Reagan's lap
Pencil on paper (sketchbook), 1988
6 x 8 (15.2 x 20.3)
Pat Oliphant, Courtesy of Susan Conway Carroll Gallery

87. Bush speaking to steelworkers
Caption: *'I see a kinder, gentler America, guys, where everyone owns a squash racket, where everybody's daughter has a coming-out party, where there are no liberals . . .'*
Pencil on paper (sketchbook), 1988
4 x 6 (10.3 x 15.2)
Pat Oliphant, Courtesy of Susan Conway Carroll Gallery

88. Bush and Congress in honeymoon bed
Caption: *Let the honeymoon commence.*
Pencil on paper (sketchbook), 1989
4 x 6 (10.3 x 15.2)
Pat Oliphant, Courtesy of Susan Conway Carroll Gallery

89. Bush on the tennis court
Caption: *'Hey! Did you see that? I returned his serve! I hit it right back to him! Am I a hero or what?'*
Pencil on paper (sketchbook), 1989
8 x 10 (20.3 x 25.4)
Pat Oliphant, Courtesy of Susan Conway Carroll Gallery

Sculpture

90. George Bush
Bronze, 1989
26½ x 39 x 11 (67.5 x 99.1 x 28)
Pat Oliphant, Courtesy of Susan Conway Carroll Gallery

INDEX

Page numbers *in italics* refer to captions of illustrations.